BREATH FROM HEAVEN

Armen Thomassian

***To those under my first charge
at Calgary Free Presbyterian Church,***
*these chapters flow out of my ministry to you.
Without your humility and teachableness, I might not
have addressed this subject at such length.*

———————————

*All Scripture quotations are taken from the
Authorized (King James) Version of the Bible.*

*All rights reserved. No part of this book may be
reproduced, scanned, or distributed in any printed or
electronic form without permission.*

Second Printing: 2023

Published by

sermon**audio**.com
"faith cometh by hearing"

Contents

Introduction 5

Section I: Sermons on Revival 9

    1. The Prototype of Revival 11

    2. The Promise of Revival 19

    3. The Past of Revival 27

    4. The Prayer of Revival 37

    5. The Prevention of Revival 45

    6. The Partnership of Revival 53

    7. The President of Revival 61

    8. The Patience in Revival 69

    9. The Product of Revival 77

    10. The Praise of Revival 85

Section II: Sermons on Prayer 93

    11. Earnest Call to Follow Good Men 95

    12. The Life of James Calder 103

    13. How To: The Prayer Meeting 113

Conclusion 123

Endnotes 127

Introduction

Sometimes in life you need to start over. So it was for the Ephesians. The words seem blunt, but Jesus told the church that they had "left their first love" and needed to "remember therefore from whence thou art fallen, and repent, and do the first works" (Rev. 2:1–7). They were theologically grounded, but they needed to return to their former zeal. They needed to kill sin, seek the power of the Spirit, and not rest until they had attained to the spiritual affections of former days.

I believe Jesus would say something similar to most of us. Perhaps worse. We have more money, books, seminaries, and resources than ever. Yet, most conservative, bible-believing congregations are existing in a spiritual ice age. Unconverted souls seldom come under conviction, divorce is common, pornography is rife, and too many believers are losing their children to the world.

Different solutions may be suggested to deal with these (and other) issues. But often the pendulum swings too far. Are churches taking their kids out of corporate worship? The solution is not to get rid of all biblical instruction tailored for various stages of maturity. Do we find the KJV archaic for our tastes? The solution is not to publish one hundred additional English translations. Is feminism bleeding into the Church? The solution is not to depict Jesus as a backwoods hunter who built a cabin with his bare hands and removed his own badly decayed teeth with nothing but a swig of whiskey and a pair of pliers.

No. There is a better way than a form of reactionism.

All our problems can be tied to spiritual decay and the departure of God. What is the solution? Revival and reformation.

Reformation without revival requires coercion. Revival without reformation lacks direction. We need a reformation that flows out of a genuine spiritual revival, where people willingly embrace all the Word of God for all of life.

This book addresses revival. By addressing this subject, I do not wish to underestimate the blessings of the ordinary means of grace. Nor do I appeal to Finney-like revivalism or carnal fanaticism. Nor do I advocate for the excesses that sometimes attend even genuine revivals. In a fallen world, man and Satan will find a way to corrupt everything good. Jonathan Edwards said,

> "If many delusions of Satan appear, at the same time that a great religious concern prevails, it is not an argument that the work in general is not the work of God, any more than it was an argument in Egypt, that there were no true miracles wrought there, by the hand of God, because Jannes and Jambres wrought false miracles at the same time by the hand of the devil."[1]

Nevertheless, there have been movements falsely named 'revivals.' Such are discerned by their emphasis on healings, dreams, ecstatic experiences, and a neglect of biblical preaching.

True revival is simply a distinct time of refreshment in the life of a Christian, a church, a community, or beyond. It is a sovereign unleashing of divine power that results in unusual degrees of spiritual life. This leads to more preaching, prayer, evangelism, and godly living. Despite counterfeits, Scottish Presbyterian John Bonar was right when he noted, "there are times when a revival is more instantly required, and should be more anxiously sought."[2]

I believe we are in such a time. Revival has shaped our past. Now it must change our present by showing us what we should pray for and how. For that reason, I commend this volume to you.

The idea to publish this work was, in God's providence, born in a prayer meeting on September 2, 2022. Amidst discussion, I was asked if I could turn my sermon series on revival into a book by the end of the month. I tried, and what you hold in your hand is the result. The title reflects a prayer that many saints of a bygone age used to pray. The fact that it is seldom heard today exposes a sad truth—namely, we not only have lost a sense of what revival is, we barely know how to pray for it.

If just one line in these pages puts you on your knees to cry out "revive thy work" (Hab. 3:2), God will have answered my prayers for this book.

Rev. Armen Thomassian
October 2022

Section I:
Sermons on Revival

This section contains a series of sermons on the topic of Revival preached during the summer of 2016.

CHAPTER 1

The Prototype of Revival

*And Adam knew his wife again; and she bare a son,
and called his name Seth: For God, said she,
hath appointed me another seed instead of Abel,
whom Cain slew. And to Seth, to him also there was
born a son; and he called his name Enos: then began
men to call upon the name of the LORD.*

Genesis 4:25-26

If you have ever seen revival advertised, it is evidence that people do not know what revival is. Revival meetings, revival weeks, revival services, have nothing to do with revival. An evangelistic campaign is not revival. Nor is a conference or a special season of prayer.

When we speak of revival, we refer to a sovereign act of God that breathes spiritual life into an area. Duncan Campbell said, "a revival is a community saturated with God."[3] The same man saw God move in extraordinary ways, not the least of which was the Isle of Lewis revival in the late 1940s. I encourage you to listen to the audio recording of him retelling his experience of the revival.

Although the Bible does not define periods of national spiritual recovery or spiritual advance as revival, such times are undoubtedly recorded, and coincide with prayer and a manifestation of the presence of God.

Unfortunately, when the average Christian speaks of the presence of God today, often it is nothing more than *frisson*, i.e. the same experience you have when you hear Handel's *Hallelujah Chorus* sung live and the hairs on the back of your neck stand on end.

The feelings experienced by many Christians during a Sunday worship production are not the same as meeting with God. Creating a hypnotic ambience and asking vulnerable people to respond to your appeals is not the same as a move of God. It is theater. If you took away the emotive music and altar call aimed at your vulnerabilities, you would feel nothing. The techniques used in modern churches work the same on people, whether done in the name of God or not.

Campbell's experience was not confined to church services. It was God saturating a community. It brings a sense of awe over an entire locality. The same is true of every other revival.

Revival is not organized. Yet, there is no separating it from earnest prayer. In a 1910 publication, Presbyterian minister Arthur T. Pierson said:

> "From the day of Pentecost, there has been not one great spiritual awakening in any land which has not begun in a union of prayer, though only among two or three; no such outward, upward movement has continued after such prayer meetings have declined; and it is in exact

proportion to the maintenance of such joint and believing supplication and intercession that the Word of the Lord in any land or locality has had free course and been glorified."[4]

Revival begins when at least one man has a burden for a visitation of God and agonizes in prayer. These men are rare. They feel the darkness, dearth, and depravity of their day, and they know only God is the answer. They seek not that God might fill empty pews and empty churches, but as Leonard Ravenhill put it, that God would fill empty hearts.

When it comes, often—such as in the 1859 revival in Northern Ireland—there is a stemming of the tide of sin. Bars empty, distilleries close, crime is greatly reduced, and people know God is working.[5]

We must understand what true revival is so that we know what we mean when we talk about it and pray for it. And we begin with the first revival. We refer to it as a *prototype* since it is the preliminary model which sets the pattern.

1. It Has a Man of God

What is the origin of this man? The end of Genesis 4 follows the tragic event between Cain and Abel. Adam and Eve have to endure the death of one son and the departure of another. But when Adam is 130 years old (Gen. 5:3), God gives another son. His name is Seth, meaning "appointed." It would appear that Adam believed

Seth was appointed by God, not merely to be a faithful son like Abel, but to be the line that leads to Christ.

In its essence, spiritual life and revival begin by leading men to Christ. It is not the purpose of God's man merely to stir people up, but to fill them with a desire for Jesus Christ. Revival is not a vain spiritual experience or an opportunity to draw attention to yourself. Revival is Christ occupying His rightful place in a community, and the man God uses always has that as his goal. This happened in the first century, when the apostles were witnesses for Christ.

Like the apostles, Seth had to serve his generation. What a generation it was. Although God banished Cain (Gen. 4:16), the achievements of Cain and his descendants are nothing short of remarkable.

This is a reminder of what man can accomplish without God. Just as Cain learned to build cities without God, so men have learned to build churches without God. But Seth is God's man to build a community that prioritizes the glory of God rather than the glory of man.

ii. It Has a Message From God

Seth lives in a generation focused on self. So, when he has a son, Seth calls him Enos, meaning "man." Various Hebrew words are translated "man" but this particular word reflects man's mortality.

In the midst of a generation that lives for hundreds of years, Seth reminds everyone that man is not immortal. Though we do not live as long in our day, we still need this reminder. All of God's greatest servants are conscious of their mortality.

So, Seth calls his son Enos to remind everyone that the curse of death is still functioning in the world. He would not let them easily forget that life is brief and all men die.

As wicked as he is, naturally there is much to admire about Cain. Cain is a hard worker. He has drive, vision, ambition, and an ability to execute projects that are unique in his world. But this is all for self. He does not name the city something that communicates God's truth. It is about his own legacy (Gen. 4:17).

This spirit of self-gratification rules in our own day. The typical professing Christian rarely asks, "what does the Lord want?" So they avoid Sunday evening services, prayer meetings, and using their gifts in God's work. The top "Christian books" and the most popular "Christian preachers" sell the same self-centered garbage that the world sells, only garnished in Christian lingo. It is humanistic, man-worshiping drivel, and it is a blight upon the Christian Church. Where are the lowly lovers of Jesus Christ who believe their only purpose is to glorify God (Rev. 4:11)?

Besides their selfishness, Seth's generation refined their skills to support their personal advancement. These things have their place. But Paul instructs Timothy in the value of exercising yourself in godliness. It profits not only now, but in the life which is to come (1 Tim. 4:8). We must do our work, but do it with the goal of receiving the approval of God.

Ultimately, Seth is directing his message of man's mortality to a sinful people. Again, consider Cain, and how he flaunts his rebellion. He appears to build a city on the doorstep of Eden where God placed the cherubim as if to justify himself before God (Gen. 3:24; 4:16). Then there is Lamech. He becomes the first polygamist, distorting God's original intention. He then writes a song celebrating sin (Gen. 4:23–24). This is what goes on in a world that needs revival.

Seth had a message that confronted these people. Yet, we live in an age when many preachers and seminary professors align with the wicked. They enjoy Lamech's music, and sing carnal lyrics as if God had made no difference between His people and the world. God help us! We need men like Seth.

No man has ever been in the heart of a revival while trifling with the entertainment of this world. Our prayers for revival are futile if we are not prepared to put away carnal pleasures. Those that make the sacrifice to abandon empty pursuits, like Seth, remind the world of man's mortality and accountability to God.

III. It Has a Move From God

Coinciding with the birth of Enos and the reminder of man's mortality, God begins to work (Gen. 4:26). Men begin to call upon God.

To "call upon" God is to worship God. No doubt Adam and Eve worshiped God, and they taught their children to worship God. But this is different. Jesus echoed the prophet Isaiah and taught that His people, gathered in His house, would be marked by prayer (Isa. 56:7; Mark 11:17). They cry to Him, desire Him, and long for Him.

Men calling upon God is the great need and the essential mark of revival. And the lack of such men and women is the blight of our day. Where are the pastors that pray like Joseph Alleine? We are told that "from four till eight he spent in prayer, holy contemplation, and singing of psalms."[6] Do such men exist today? Indeed, where are the churches that pray together, and where are the Christians that are spiritually sensitive enough to note the departure of God, and spiritually determined enough to seek for Him?

Moreover, when they called upon the name of the Lord, it was a proof of their conversion. During Peter's sermon on the day of Pentecost, he quotes from Joel 2, "And it shall come to pass, that whosoever shall call on the name of the Lord shall be saved" (Acts 2:21).

The thousands converted that day called upon God, and they kept on calling upon God (Acts 2:42). But where are these people today? We have thousands of churches and few that pray. Is this not a sign of sickness? Is not prayerlessness a tragic evidence of man's departure from God and God's departure from man?

But it does not stop there. To call upon God is to consecrate yourself to God. We see this in the life of Abraham. His calling upon God is often paired with building an altar of sacrifice. Abraham was willing to offer his most prized possessions to God as he prayed (Gen. 12:8; 22:2; 26:25). He was consecrated to God.

E. M. Bounds said, "Our praying, however, needs to be pressed and pursued with an energy that never tires, a persistency which will not be denied, and a courage that never fails."[7]

Revival never comes by wishing, only by praying. The soil that often sprouts a genuine revival is one where men bring themselves to the cross of Christ and consecrate themselves to God. Then they stay there. Day after day, week after week, and month after month they pray and yearn for God until the Spirit is poured forth. This being the case, are you surprised there is no revival in your community and mine?

CHAPTER 2

The Promise of Revival

*If my people, which are called by my name,
shall humble themselves, and pray, and seek my face,
and turn from their wicked ways; then will I hear
from heaven, and will forgive their sin,
and will heal their land.*

2 Chronicles 7:14

No religious temple was ever like Solomon's Temple. Its beauty, extravagance, and splendor were unparalleled among earthly structures.

At its dedication, Solomon addresses the people with a brief history, then offers one of the most lengthy prayers in all the Bible (2 Chron. 6:12–42). And what a prayer it is. Israel was in its greatest time of power, peace, and prosperity. Yet Solomon has foresight to know the future would be different (2 Chron. 6:26–31).

After the prayer, something happens that Israel had not seen since the commencement of tabernacle worship (Lev. 9:22–24). God comes, fire consumes the sacrifice, and everyone falls on their faces. The presence of God is so palpable that the priests "could not enter into the house of the Lord" (2 Chron. 7:1–2).

As unusual as it seems, God has humbled men by His presence throughout history. During America's First Great Awakening, Jonathan Edwards preached, 'Sinners in the Hands of an Angry God.' Referring to this occasion in 1741, in which Edwards had been invited to Enfield, we are told:

> "One of these instances, which occurred at Enfield, at a time of great religious indifference there, is thus mentioned by the Rev. Dr. Trumbull. 'When they went into the meeting-house, the appearance of the assembly was thoughtless and vain. The people hardly conducted themselves with common decency. The Rev Mr. Edwards, of Northampton, preached; and before the sermon was ended, the assembly appeared deeply impressed, and bowed down with an awful conviction of their sin and danger. There was such a breathing of distress and weeping, that the preacher was obliged to speak to the people and desire silence, that he might be heard.' This was the commencement of a general and powerful revival of religion."[8]

Some oppose praying for such outpourings of the Spirit. Others believe if Christians meet all the requirements, God must send a revival. Both are wrong. George Whitefield—who may be the greatest preacher the English-speaking world has ever seen—saw tremendous evidence of God's power during his first visit to America. But subsequent visits did not see the same effects. Charles

Spurgeon's ministry is similar. Though his preaching improved and the church grew, the greatest outpouring of power was in his earlier years. God is sovereign, and the measure of His blessing is in His hands.

While spoken in the context of the nation of Israel, 2 Chronicles 7:14 was "written for our learning" (Rom. 15:4). The glory of Solomon's Temple was a foreshadowing of God's most glorious tabernacle of all, Jesus Christ in union with His people. Solomon acknowledges, "But will God in very deed dwell with men on the earth? behold, heaven and the heaven of heavens cannot contain thee; how much less this house which I have built!" (2 Chron. 6:18). But in the New Testament, Paul says, "In him dwelleth all the fulness of the Godhead bodily" (Col. 2:9). Christ is the foundation of the greatest tabernacle, with His people joined to Him as a living structure and dwelling place of the Spirit (Eph. 2:20-22; 1 Pet. 2:5).

Solomon could pray this prayer for his kingdom. Are we to suggest that Israel had a greater king than Jesus, and access to greater promises and favor? Is the death and resurrection of Christ of no consequence to the blessing of God upon men? 2 Chronicles 7:14 is a model and affords encouragement to the Israel of God. Let us consider the instruction of this text.

1. The Recipients of the Promise

Solomon understood that sin shuts heaven. And he feared the day that God would prevent the rain and cause a famine. But while not all sin prevents physical rain, sin that God's people knowingly harbor in their hearts will always shut heaven to their prayers.

Do you feel a deadness in prayer? Does prayer seem pointless? This may be the issue. Solomon desired God to give attention to "any man" that would confess sin (2 Chron. 6:29). So God promises, "If my people…" We have a habit of looking at how things are and blaming politicians, policies, and preachers. But this promise obligates each Christian to take responsibility for the spiritual climate of their generation.

Often, the national issues reflect a deeper issue within the Church. Isaiah 1:9 shows that the faithful remnant can preserve the nation from becoming like Sodom. God does not say, if my priests, or pastors, or prophets… He says, "If my people…" Church history shows that it doesn't always come through the leaders. Often it is a small group of believers that are more *concerned* than they are *critical*. More given to *prayer* than *protesting*. And God sees their spirit and fervency.

II. The Requirements of the Promise

The first requirement is *humility*, "shall humble themselves." Whatever difficulty there is in prayer, the greater difficulty is in humbling yourself. The foundation of all spiritual poverty is pride. The declension of any church or denomination begins with pride.

Many of us find ourselves in churches and denominations where the slide into spiritual bankruptcy is well under way. We can either accept it, complain about it, blame others for it, or humble ourselves and get to serious prayer.

When a church or denomination has known uncommon blessings in its past, the memory of that blessing becomes a blindfold. We become like Israel, and God has to say, "but my people know not the judgment of the LORD" (Jer. 8:7). We say in our pride that we have known blessing. Our fathers were these great preachers. We can mark the hand of God upon our church. We still hold to the same truths. We conduct the same practices. Everything is the same.

Except it is not. The tender-hearted know that God has withdrawn the marked evidence of His presence. The problem? Pride.

The second requirement is *importunity*, "pray and seek my face." Importunity is the ability to persist almost to the point of annoyance. Christ encourages this kind of praying (Luke 11:8; 18:5). The multiplying of terms, i.e. pray and seek, reflects this attitude of persistence. But what does it mean to seek the face of God? In the Old Testament, the Hebrew word for "seek" is often translated "presence."

Thus, the aim of such praying is to enjoy the presence of God. We can enjoy this on an individual level, which is why we should desire personal revival at the very least. Nothing gladdens the believer more than an evident sense of God's presence. Are you enjoying God's presence? Can it be said of you that "thou hast made him exceeding glad with thy countenance" (Ps. 21:6)? No excuse validates our own cold hearts and distance from God.

The third requirement is *sincerity*, "turn from their wicked ways." Oh, how we need God to shine the light of His Word upon specific areas of our lives. To expose our blind spots. We need to sense the working of the Spirit and His striving in our hearts. We must rid ourselves of the little foxes that spoil the vines (Song 2:15). We must locate and remove the fly in the apothecary's ointment (Ecc. 10:1). If there is a little leaven in the lump, we must purge it immediately (1 Cor. 5:6–7).

Look for the self sins that quietly strangle the life of God in the soul. "To be specific, the self-sins are these: self-righteousness, self-pity, self-confidence, self-sufficiency, self-admiration, self-love and a host of others like them."[9] — A. W. Tozer.

Sin is the veil that blinds us to the glory of God in Christ. To quote Tozer again about self sins, "It is the veil of our fleshly fallen nature living on, unjudged within us, uncrucified and unrepudiated. It is the close-woven veil of the self-life which we have never truly acknowledged, of which we have been secretly ashamed, and which for these reasons we have never brought to the judgment of the cross."[10]

III. The Realization of the Promise

First, *there is the acknowledgment:* "then will I hear from heaven." Implying that prior to this, God had not heard. Before we question whether God is listening, let us first go back through the text and make sure we have dealt with our sin. When we do this, the heavens are often no longer like brass.

Second, *there is acceptance:* "and will forgive their sin." In Eden, Adam enjoyed the presence of God. There was no barrier between him and God because there was no sin. And while we know the cross of Christ is the answer for our sin, we must heed 1 John 1:9, "If we confess our sins, he is faithful and just to forgive us our sins, and to cleanse us from all unrighteousness." Do we name our besetting sins? Our specific self sins? When we get serious about confessing sin, God forgives and removes the barrier, for Christ's sake.

Third, *there is an amendment:* "and heal their land." Will God amend the spiritual condition of our nation? What about your church? Our forefathers saw it. Yet, few of us are even seeking it in earnest. Is it because we refuse to deal with secret sins?

> "The principal object of God's eye is the inward and secret frame of the soul: labor, therefore, to be cleansed from secret sins. 'If I regard iniquity in my heart, the Lord will not hear me' (Ps. 66:18). 'Behold, thou desirest truth in the inward parts' (Ps. 51:6). Therefore is He often said in Scripture to 'search the heart and reins,' which intimates His special observation of the secret frame. It is true that God gives charge against open sins. Why? Because He would not have any to be profane; and so He gives singular

charge against secret sins. Why? Because He cannot endure any to be hypocritical."[11]
— Obadiah Sedgwick (1600–1658).

Our churches are dying for want of Christians that understand how much God hates hidden and protected sins. But until we get serious about being holy vessels filled with His Spirit, we are unlikely to see the revival we desire. Not even in our own hearts.

CHAPTER 3

The Past of Revival

We have heard with our ears, O God, our fathers have told us, what work thou didst in their days, in the times of old. How thou didst drive out the heathen with thy hand, and plantedst them; how thou didst afflict the people, and cast them out.

Psalm 44

Few subjects are easier to shy away from than revival. How can you speak about something you have never experienced? While this is a lamentable reality for many of us, it is not a good reason to avoid the topic.

The Word of God is sufficient and our only rule for faith and practice. When it teaches us something, it is because God intends all His people to know about it. In this case, the Bible is filled with examples of revival. The entire book of Judges, the reign of various kings such as Hezekiah, Josiah, etc. Rather than ignoring the Church's best days, we are obligated to remind God's people what God has done in the past.

In his book, 'Land of Many Revivals,' Tom Lennie traces the extraordinary movement of the Holy Spirit in Scotland from 1527 to 1857. Page after page takes you to scenes that stir the soul. The original home of Presbyterianism is steeped in revival. Despite that, when you visit most Presbyterian churches today, it is like dining on a plate of dry bread. The form is there, but it is a far cry from what you read of early Presbyterianism.

While often depicted as staid and austere, the roots of Presbyterianism were established in a fiery baptism of spiritual power. Wave after wave of localized moves of the Spirit upended communities and put hardened sinners on their faces before God.

Church history is crucial for us to know, just as Israel's history was vital for the psalmist. It is difficult to be dogmatic regarding the precise setting of this Psalm, but it appears to be in a time of failure. Because of this, we will find it easy to feel something of the burden of the psalmist's heart.

1. The Knowledge of the Past

First, we can see that the psalmist had knowledge of the past because it was *conveyed* to him, "we have heard with our ears…" (Ps. 44:1). Previous generations were very careful to pass on their history to their children, which is important to the Lord. At the institution of the Passover we read, "And it shall come to pass, when your children shall say unto you, What mean ye by this service? That ye shall say, It is the sacrifice of the Lord's passover, who passed over the houses of the children of Israel in Egypt, when he smote the Egyptians, and delivered our houses" (Ex. 12:26–27). Each generation had an obligation to share the details of the Passover.

Sharing the victories of the Lord with others, particularly our children, is vital. In similar fashion, preachers should supplement their sermons with biblical history and church history rather than references to pop-culture.

Second, the knowledge of the past was *clarifying*. The psalmist says, "How thou didst drive out the heathen with thy hand, and plantedst them…" (Ps. 44:2–3). Here we see that the events on the mind of the psalmist are when Israel entered the Promised Land. They were a feeble people, not known for their skill in war (a fact that no doubt contributed to their unbelief at Kadesh-Barnea). Although they rightly understood their weakness, the ten spies came back with a report that ignored what God had done in the past. But, the history of God's power and promises was the very thing that encouraged the faith of Caleb and Joshua. Israel had lifted no weapon, and yet God delivered them from the hand of Egypt, the mightiest nation on earth.

Believers should use past experiences to bolster faith in the present. The most doom and gloom Christians are often those who do not know history. They imagine the darkness of the present is unprecedented and we have no grounds for hope. Hogwash! History tells us otherwise. And every so often a Joshua arises to expose our unbelief.

II. The Expectation of the Past

"Thou art my King, O God: command deliverances for Jacob. Through thee will we push down our enemies:

through thy name will we tread them under that rise up against us" (Ps. 44:4-5). See the confidence of the psalmist? He did not look back at his forefathers and attribute the success of the nation to them. That would have caused despair or generated excuses. He knew their victory was by God's power.

"For I will not trust in my bow, neither shall my sword save me. But thou hast saved us from our enemies..." (Ps. 44:6–8). History taught the psalmist to expect deliverance only from the hand of the Lord. He had no trust in his own weapons. He knew that God loves to work through deficient people, with deficient prayers, and deficient power, to prove that the work is all Him. However, we must not stop going to God for strength. Octavius Winslow points out a helpful danger:

> "There is a proneness in us to deify the graces of the Spirit. We often think of faith and love, and their kindred graces, as though they were essentially omnipotent; forgetting that though they undoubtedly are divine in their origin, spiritual in their nature, and sanctifying in their effects, they yet are sustained by no self-supporting power, but by constant communications of life and nourishment from Jesus; that, the moment of their being left to their inherent strength, is the moment of their certain declension and decay."[12]

In other words, it does not matter what we have accomplished in the past. We must continue going to the Lord to prevent the decay of our inner life, and to strengthen us as He has strengthened our forefathers. It is only then that we get to see God's "strength is made perfect in weakness" (2 Cor. 12:9).

iii. The Comparison of the Past

As the psalmist considers the past, he makes a comparison between then and now, and he notes a few things.

First, *they are devoid of God's presence.* He says God "goest not forth with our armies" (Ps. 44:9). Moses knew how much the people needed the presence of God (Ex. 33:14–16), and God promised His presence to Joshua in his conquest (Josh. 1:9). While it is commendable to rest in the promise of God's presence, we should learn from the psalmist to seek for evidence of it.

Second, *they are devoid of God's power.* He declares, "Thou makest us to turn back from the enemy…" (Ps. 44:10). They had no power to resist their enemies. Does this not illustrate us today? We have plans, programs, and philosophies for God's work, but little power to resist the enemies. Marriages are falling apart. Professing believers enjoy little victory over sin. Few churches regularly see conversions to Christ. Are we not overcome?

Third, *they are devoid of God's protection.* He laments, "Thou hast given us like sheep appointed for meat…" (Ps. 44:11). It gets worse. God does not seem to protect

His people. We feel ourselves crushed, silenced, and sometimes destroyed by the power of our enemies. What is going on? Are God's people to accept this condition?

Fourth, *they are devoid of God's purpose.* The psalmist charges God, "Thou sellest thy people for nought" (Ps. 44:12). Just as we might give away what has no value to us or serves us no purpose, so it seems God gets rid of His people for no gain.

Fifth, *they are devoid of God's preference.* He says, "Thou makest us a reproach to our neighbours, a scorn and a derision… a byword… a shaking of the head among the people" (Ps. 44:13–14). How things have changed (see v. 3). Sometimes we look back at periods of the Church and it seemed as if the favor of God was undeniable.

Mary Queen of Scots is reputed to have said, "I fear the prayers of John Knox more than all the assembled armies of Europe." This is akin to when David was on the throne, "And the fame of David went out into all lands; and the Lord brought the fear of him upon all nations" (1 Chron. 14:17). Where is this preferential favor upon the Church today?

IV. The Faithfulness of the Past

What is strange about the condition of the nation from the psalmist's perspective is that they had stayed true to the Lord (Ps. 44:17–18). There was no glaring sin. It appears they had been overcome despite their faithfulness.

Events that appear to frustrate the advancement of the Church are not uncommon. With the death of many martyrs, there can be a feeling of defeat. Such believers can look at God and say, "Our heart is not turned back, neither have our steps declined from thy way" (Ps. 44:18).

Can we say this? Has the world crept in and laid a claim upon our affections? Or are we like those in Jeremiah's day, who "have committed two evils; they have forsaken me the fountain of living waters, and hewed them out cisterns, broken cisterns, that can hold no water" (Jer. 2:13). If there has been a diminishing of your zeal from the past, why? Is God less worthy than He was when your zeal was at its height? If we cannot secure revival, let us at least be faithful.

v. The Repetition of the Past

The psalmist closes with a prayer, and what a prayer it is (Ps. 44:23–26). Having laid out God's deliverance in the past, he brings an earnest request for a repeat of the past. Note the language, "awake… arise… redeem."

Does God sleep? No, but it feels like it to the psalmist. He does not allow his theology to prevent him from praying what he feels. Though we should be reverent and careful, God invites us to pour out our hearts and reflect where we are.

The question remains, why does God allow His people to suffer at the hands of evil men? Paul helps us to understand why when he quotes from Psalm 44 in Romans 8:36. The suffering of God's people is "for thy sake." Paul concludes that suffering is the experience of the Church in every age. Even in times when God's power is evident, evil men lead Stephen (Acts 7) and James (Acts 12) as lambs to the slaughter. We may go through "tribulation, or distress, or persecution, or famine, or nakedness, or peril, or sword" and yet "in all these things we are more than conquerors through him that loved us" (Rom. 8:35–37).

The inevitability of suffering is not a reason to resign ourselves to circumstances. Examine the prayer of Acts 4:24–31, and you will see it echo the prayer of the psalmist. Enemies have arrayed themselves against the Lord and His people. The duty of the Church is to keep preaching with boldness, and God equipped them by pouring out the Holy Spirit.

Archibald Glover, who served in China with the Hudson Taylor's China Inland Mission, once said,

> "Did the Word anywhere teach that God's servants were ever to accept defeat at the hands of Satan? Assuredly not. Had Satan at any time succeeded through persecution in destroying the cause of Christ? Far from it.... Paul, the great missionary, testified that the persecutions which befell him had "fallen out rather unto the progress of the gospel," and he followed on to exhort his fellow workers to be "in nothing terrified by your adversaries." Nothing in the New Testament missionary record is more impressive than the way opposition and

persecution from the enemy were repeatedly made by God the very means of advancing the missionary enterprise. Every such assault of the adversary today, therefore, should become the occasion of a forward movement issuing in fresh expansion and enlarged results."[13]

Revival is not hindered by persecution. Though faithful saints can feel abandoned, exposed to enemies, and even pay with the price of their own life, these trials stimulate more fervent prayer and greater outpourings of the Spirit that advance the Gospel.

The brightest days for the Church have come, not just on the back of dark times, but often in the midst of them. Like the psalmist, we have every right to fortify our faith with evidence of spiritual awakenings from the past. When sin abounds, and the ominous clouds of persecution come rolling in, let us storm the battlements of the enemy with persistent, believing prayer.

CHAPTER 4

The Prayer of Revival

*Wilt thou not revive us again:
that thy people may rejoice in thee?*

Psalm 85:6

No other organization on the face of the earth has the same guarantee of success as the Church of Jesus Christ. Christ promised, "I **will** build my church" (Matt. 16:18).

He knew there would be opposition, but it would never—and will never—prevail against His purpose. The one who made the worlds and man from the dust, exercises His omnipotence in building His Church. If we are at ease in Zion (Amos 6:1), He is not.

Thus, if the wickedness of the world is greater now than in previous generations, we should expect Christ to give more grace and unction. He will not permit His Church to flounder in the face of its enemies. This is not our mission; it is Christ's mission. The goal, the end, the desire to advance His kingdom is His. Even so, if we see the Church struggling, we have a responsibility to seek God for a manifestation of power to push it forward (Mark 9:29).

Despite signs of declension in the Church, many professing Christians live day to day like atheists. They wake up like an atheist, and get washed, dressed, and go to work never committing their day to God. Such habits prove our spiritual coldness. Though Christ will build His Church, it will not be with cold believers. That would be like asking the hospitalized to help build a new extension to the hospital.

But that is not the psalmist. He is looking back to a more favorable time. "Lord, thou hast been favourable unto thy land… Thou hast forgiven the iniquity of thy people, thou hast covered all their sin" (Ps. 86:1–3).

What more could we want for ourselves? God has been favorable and forgiven our sin. Yet, the psalmist senses the anger of God (v. 5) and the cry of his heart is, "Wilt thou not revive us again: that thy people may rejoice in thee?" (Ps. 85:6).

1. The Reason for the Prayer

These were a favored people (v. 1). All God's people are favored people. None of us have done anything to deserve the goodness and mercy of God. Yet, far too often we are as those described by Octavius Winslow:

> "If there is one consideration more humbling than another to a spiritually-minded believer, it is, that, after all God has done for him,—after all the rich displays of his grace, the patience and tenderness of his instructions, the repeated

discipline of his covenant, the tokens of love received, and the lessons of experience learned, there should still exist in the heart a principle, the tendency which is to secret, perpetual, and alarming departure from God."[14]

Is this not the sin of the Ephesians who left their first love (Rev. 2:4)? So the psalmist prays that God would restrain His judgment by turning their hearts, "Turn us, O God of our salvation, and cause thine anger toward us to cease..." (Ps. 85:4–5).

He also indicates that they had turned to folly (Ps. 85:8). In such times, God's people need direct words, such as those issued by the Presbytery on the Isle of Lewis a few months before revival broke out:

> "The Presbytery of Lewis having taken into consideration the low state of vital religion within their own bounds, and throughout the land generally, call upon their faithful people in all their congregations to take serious view of the present dispensation of divine displeasure manifested, not only in the chaotic conditions of international politics and morality but also, and especially, in the lack of spiritual power from Gospel ordinances, and to realize that these things plainly indicate that the Most High has a controversy with the nation... The Presbytery affectionately plead with their people—especially with the youth of the

church—to take these matters to heart and to make serious inquiry as to what must be the end, should there be no repentance; and they call upon every individual as before God to examine his or her heart in the light of that responsibility which pertains to us all, that haply, in the divine mercy, we may be visited with the spirit of repentance and may turn again unto the Lord whom we have so grieved with our iniquities and waywardness. Especially would they warn the young people of the devil's man-traps—the cinema and the public-house [bar]."[15] — Free Church Presbytery of Lewis, 1949.

Nowadays, such an exhortation to self-examination, abandoning the world, and repentance would be met with ridicule in many churches. Some, with little regard for their spiritual life and little thought for the dangers of the world, would—in derogatory tones—label it 'pietism.' With a cigar in one hand and a glass of bourbon in the other, they would cast aside these elders and their exhortations to repentance and holiness. I pity such people. For it was to the Isle of Lewis that God would come. Months later, the Lord honored their appeal with a mighty revival.

Would to God there were more spiritual watchmen like this in our day. Men who sense the "present dispensation of divine displeasure." If good men called for repentance in rural Scotland in 1949, what would they say in our context today? In a Church desensitized to porn, violence, divorce, murder, and idolatries of various kinds, we need exhortations like these.

Is not God displeased with our half-heartedness? Is He not displeased with our reluctance to commune with Him? I can hear the defensive retort that says the work of Christ means God is never displeased with His people. Is this true?

First, there is a difference between the eternal wrath of God and the displeasure of a loving Father. Second, it is easy to prove His displeasure towards His indifferent people. Jesus sent a warning of divine displeasure to a first century church, "I know thy works, that thou art neither cold nor hot: I would thou wert cold or hot. So then because thou art lukewarm, and neither cold nor hot, I will spue thee out of my mouth" (Rev. 3:15–16).

Do not try to justify your life by the deteriorating standards of your environment. Preachers, do not take your cue from the example of cold, dead academics that rarely share the Gospel. Nor should you follow the example of politically-driven men. With few exceptions, such individuals think the biggest threat to the Church is cancel culture, when the reality is more likely to be canceled prayer.

Judgment must begin with God's people at the house of God (1 Pet. 4:17), and the psalmist knows the need is deeper repentance.

II. The Request in the Prayer

The word "revive" is used over 200 times in the Old Testament, and is most often translated 'to live.'

And that is what revival is. When God visits, He comes with an infusion of new life. "My soul cleaveth unto the dust: quicken [revive] thou me according to thy word" (Ps. 119:25).

This burden for revival is common among men of the past. Robert Murray M'Cheyne was a pastor who desired revival. He ministered in Dundee for several years before his death at 29. On Thursday evenings, he conducted a prayer meeting. It was here where he would share various historical accounts of revival.[16] This continued for a couple of years, and while the church enjoyed a measure of blessing, there was no revival.

When M'Cheyne left for six months to visit the Holy Land, he appointed William Chalmers Burns to fill the pulpit. During this time, Burns visited his father's church in Kilsyth to help oversee a communion season. God was pleased to visit Kilsyth with a breath of the Spirit. When Burns returned to Dundee from Kilsyth, the power and blessing of God appeared to follow, and revival broke out in M'Cheyne's congregation. While He used someone else, God answered M'Cheyne's prayer for revival. God awakened His people, saved hundreds of souls, and such was the hunger in the community, meetings had to be held every evening.

Can you imagine such a hunger for God in your church? The psalmist is praying for God to enliven His people. He senses the spiritual deadness, which leads to joylessness. Thus, he prays for new life in order that "thy people may rejoice in thee."

There has never been a move of God without a concerted effort in prayer. David M'Intyre, near the close of his book, *The Hidden Life of Prayer*, noted, "In a word, every gracious work which has been accomplished within the kingdom of God has been begun, fostered and consummated by prayer."

Some like the idea of revival. But few will pay the price. The price of time invested in prayer. And no ordinary prayer, or complacent prayer, but fervent prayer.

III. The Result of the Prayer

Throughout vv. 8–13, the psalmist reflects hope for the future and an anticipation of how the Lord would answer his prayer. In the middle of it, he gives a prophecy concerning the Messiah, "Mercy and truth are met together; righteousness and peace have kissed each other" (Ps. 85:10). There is only one place where mercy and truth meet together: in Christ.

Truth calls us sinners and drives us from God. Mercy calls us children and brings us near to God. This is the redemptive work of Christ. Our failed obedience should bring the wrath of God, but Christ's righteousness gives us the peace of God.

Following verse 10 is a series of blessings that Christ brings to pass (vv. 11–13), culminating in the expectation that Christ's work "shall set us in the way of his steps," i.e. will make us walk as Christ walked (1 John 2:6).

Revival is an unusual work of the Spirit that rapidly advances Christ-likeness in men. It strengthens us to bear a greater burden for the kingdom and results in sudden blessings upon the Church.

When the aforementioned William Chalmers Burns preached in Kilsyth in July 1839, God worked suddenly. His text was Psalm 110:3, "Thy people shall be willing in the day of thy power." Conviction fell upon the assembly, and a work was done in many hearts.

When he returned to Kilsyth in September, there was clear evidence of the Spirit's influence. Nightly prayer meetings were being held, and sin had been visibly suppressed in the community. During this second visit, a 7 p.m. evening service did not conclude until 3 a.m., and Burns had to counsel the distressed of soul until 6 a.m. God visited that small town.

This is revival. It is a visitation of God. A visitation in answer to prayer.

CHAPTER 5

THE PREVENTION OF REVIVAL

*Behold, the LORD'S hand is not shortened,
that it cannot save; neither his ear heavy,
that it cannot hear: But your iniquities have separated
between you and your God, and your sins have hid his
face from you, that he will not hear.*

ISAIAH 59:1-2

Dr. Martyn Lloyd-Jones noted that in revival, cardinal truths are crucial.[17] He claimed there had never been a revival among Unitarians or Roman Catholics, because belief in doctrines like the deity of Christ and justification by faith alone were necessary before you had any hope of an outpouring of the Spirit. The Protestant Reformation occurred in part because Luther proclaimed a biblical view of justification. The same is true of the Methodist movement. Right doctrine is foundational to spiritual awakening.

But one may own and proclaim the truth and yet not enjoy anything of God's power and presence. We can find one reason in this passage in which God addresses the professing church.

The imagery is anthropomorphic. Literally speaking, God has no hand, ear, or face. God is Spirit. Furthermore, since God is omnipresent, He cannot hide Himself from His creation. So when it refers to God hiding His face, it reflects the removal of His favor.

I assume you do not want that. But rather, you want to see evidence of God's ear open to you and His arm ready to move in answer to your prayers. So why is it not happening?

A. W. Tozer is reputed to have said, "Revival will come when prayer is no longer used as a substitute for obedience." This drives home an important truth. The same truth Isaiah addressed.

1. The False Assumption

We might assume that the reason God removed His favor was because of the lack of prayer. However, the passage shows that the people are engaging in worship and that they have some interest in spiritual activity. But they are hypocrites. They may pray, but even their fasting had wrong motives. The Lord calls them to exercise their religion in purity of heart (Isa. 58:1–9). They drew near with their mouth and lips, but their heart was far from God (Isa. 29:13).

And though they felt righteous, they were far from it. Their society was filled with injustice and their feet ran to evil (Isa. 59:3–4, vv. 7–8). God sees their wickedness, but the people do not. John Gill, the English Baptist pastor of the 18th century, said:

> "Like a partition wall dividing between them, so that they enjoy no communion with him in his worship and ordinances; which is greatly the case of the reformed churches: they profess the true God, and the worship of him, and do attend the outward ordinances of it; but this is done in such a cold formal way, and such sins and wickedness are perpetrated and connived at, that the Lord does not grant his gracious presence to them, but stands at a distance from them."[18]

Is it not the same today? We can be swift to point out the error in other churches, but there is often a cold formality in our own Bible-believing churches. And in the secret parts of our lives, our feet run to evil and our "thoughts are thoughts of iniquity."

Then, we ascribe the lack of divine power to the sovereignty of God. Yes, God is sovereign. But this is a convenient truth for those who refuse to seek spiritual awakening. The problem is not with God's hand or God's ear. That is an assumption. The problem is with the people. Our day is no different.

ii. The Biblical Apprehension

How do we biblically apprehend what prevents revival? There are always consequences for actions, but Paul reminds God's people, "Whatsoever a man soweth, that shall he also reap" (Gal. 6:7–8). Every day you sow. The question is, what are you sowing? And since we reap what we sow, does this give an indication as to why God does not hear our prayers? The fact that God hides His face from His people is not an isolated event: "Then my anger shall be kindled against them in that day, and I will forsake them, and I will hide my face from them, and they shall be devoured, and many evils and troubles shall befall them; so that they will say in that day, Are not these evils come upon us, because our God is not among us?" (Deut. 31:17). See also Deut. 28:23; Hosea 5:6–7.

Why does God hide? It is simple. **God stops listening to you when you stop listening to Him.** If you sow the practice of ignoring God, you reap the consequence of God ignoring you. Historically, God's people have struggled to hear and obey God as they should (Isa. 30:9; Jer. 22:21).

Jesus teaches the importance of listening to God if we want Him to listen to us when He said, "If ye abide in me, and my words abide in you, ye shall ask what ye will, and it shall be done unto you" (John 15:7). It is as if Jesus is saying, if you listen to me and do, then I will listen to you and do. It is a simple principle. If you want God to ignore you, ignore Him. If you want God to hear you, hear Him.

We cannot excuse our shortcomings. Even our "thoughts of iniquity." We must be sensitive to all the revealed will of God. The psalmist understood this: "If I regard iniquity in my heart, the Lord will not hear me" (Ps. 66:18).

The God-sent preacher that points people away from the world is mocked as an ascetic. The one who argues that the inner life matters is slandered as a mystic. This is why our churches are powerless and carnal. We will not acknowledge that there is—and I say this carefully—a human element to revival. The instruments used by God in His sovereign providence, do not trifle with sin. I do not mean to say they are without sin, that is impossible. But, they wage constant war against anything that hinders their inner life, or threatens to rob them of spiritual power.

III. The Gospel Answer

The language of these verses brings to mind God's power when He delivered His people from Egypt. The entire picture of the Exodus is one of Gospel significance because the people never lifted a weapon. And it began when God's ear was not heavy (Ex. 2:23–24), and His arm was not shortened (Ex. 6:6; Deut. 7:19). It culminates in the Passover, pointing to the blood of Christ as the only basis for deliverance. In other words, it is the blood of Christ that demands the ear of God and puts into action the arm of God for salvation.

Nevertheless, God expects His people to obey His commandments. Whatever we might say of our dependence on the work of Christ, God's genuine children obey: "And whatsoever we ask, we receive of him, because we keep his commandments, and do those things that are pleasing in his sight" (1 John 3:22). Obedience is not the grounds of answered prayer, but it is the evidence of a justified person. God demands and His Spirit produces ongoing faith and repentance. Unconfessed and unforsaken sin breaks fellowship with God. We must repudiate any sin that the Spirit puts His finger upon.

In the 1700s, England saw a rise of Deism, the belief that God made all things but disassociated Himself from His creation.[19] This helped to drive people from true Christianity and gave them a license to sin. The Bible was cast aside, and the country fell headlong into more and more corruption. What was God's answer? Social reform? A new political party?

The answer was found in a handful of men that the world derided. Known as "The Holy Club," the group included John and Charles Wesley, as well as George Whitefield. Though initially unconverted, they were extremely diligent about living a pious life. But the power of their ministry was not evident until they knew and preached the Gospel of salvation by grace alone.

When a man lives devoted to God and preaches the Gospel of justifying grace through the merits of Christ, untold good can come of it. We have the message. But do we also have a pious and prayerful devotion that drives us to deal with unforsaken sin?

English Puritan George Swinnock said,

"When the sin of the petitioner is before God's eyes his petitions cannot enter into God's ears; the wide mouth of sin outcrieth the voice of his prayers… the smallest sin, loved and liked, will hinder the course of prayer, though it be never so instant and vehement... Men by falls sometimes lose their speeches, men by sin lose their prayers."[20]

If you are a praying saint, do not be like those in Isaiah's day. Do not simply hear the Word. Obey it. Peter warns husbands to treat their wives as God requires, "that your prayers be not hindered" (1 Pet. 3:7). We must not tolerate any compromise or light-hearted views of sin. The path we are called to is: listen, do, repent, repeat. Every day. And even if you do not live to see a great revival, is not Christ worthy of your devotion? Even without the promise of anything in return?

CHAPTER 6

The Partnership of Revival

*Behold, how good and how pleasant it is for
brethren to dwell together in unity! It is like the
precious ointment upon the head, that ran down upon
the beard, even Aaron's beard: that went down to the
skirts of his garments; As the dew of Hermon, and as
the dew that descended upon the mountains of Zion:
for there the LORD commanded the blessing,
even life for evermore.*

Psalm 133

Following Psalm 119, there is a collection of 15 psalms with the title 'A song of degrees' or 'A psalm of ascent.' Scholars believe these psalms were grouped together because Jews sang them on their way to Jerusalem to worship. In contrast to the psalms that are more focused on the penman's personal experience, the theme in these psalms is a longing for the good of the nation.

The history of Israel is one of turmoil and division. However, at various times, Israel enjoyed great harmony.

When David took the throne we are told, "Then all Israel gathered themselves to David unto Hebron, saying,

Behold, we are thy bone and thy flesh" (1 Chron. 11:1). This Psalm expresses the desire for such a day of unity.

The Psalm begins with "Behold…" i.e. listen! The Spirit of God draws our attention to the importance of the subject matter. God's people are to dwell in unity. This is reinforced by the Westminster Confession,

> "Saints by profession are bound to maintain a holy fellowship and communion in the worship of God… Which communion, as God offereth opportunity, is to be extended unto all those who, in every place, call upon the name of the Lord Jesus" (WCF 26.2).

But why deal with this in our consideration of revival? Because God's blessing is never known where grudges are held and schism exists.

In every instance of revival, despite humble beginnings, there is a heightened sense of the call to unity. A nucleus of believers seeking God for His blessing can have no tolerance for sectarianism. Separate, yes, but not sectarian.

1. The Preciousness of the Partnership

The psalmist does not remark on the pleasantness of *all* men dwelling in unity. It is specifically "brethren." Should we not expect unity among those whom God has saved? They are cleansed by the same blood, sanctified by the same Spirit, instructed by the same Word, and baptized into the same body.

Yet there are some who barely agree with themselves, never mind other believers. And whether stated or not, they appreciate unity only with those who are the same as them. They enjoy finding differences among brethren more than establishing common ground.

Do not misunderstand me. Is there a place for identifying damaging personalities within the professed church? Absolutely. But, it is one thing to be willing to mark false teachers. It is another thing entirely when that is how people will remember you. Such individuals practice a form of monasticism, isolating themselves—not from the world—but from the body of Christ. This is wrong. Unity should not require uniformity. We must fight to suppress pride, and delight in fellowship with genuine, blood-washed believers.

Of course, those guilty of schismatic attitudes always have arguments to justify themselves. Like Hyper-Calvinists that use the doctrine of election to cover their lack of evangelism, divisive brethren use the legitimate doctrine of separation to mask their estrangement from God's people. They demand characteristics that stretch the requirements of Scripture and narrow the Church like foolish disciples (Mark 9:38).

Have we not learned from the father of the faithful? When strife breaks out between the herdsmen of Abraham and Lot, Abraham is wise to do everything in his power to bring peace. He knew that "the Canaanite and the Perizzite dwelled then in the land" (Gen. 13:7).

It is almost as if Abraham took to heart the words of our Lord in John 13:34-35, "A new commandment I give unto you, That ye love one another; as I have loved you, that ye also love one another. By this shall all men know that ye are my disciples, if ye have love one to another." The psalmist is no different. He viewed time spent in unity with brethren as "good and pleasant."

Is that how you feel towards God's people? Even those with whom you have differences?

The psalmist says it is "like the precious ointment upon the head" (v. 2). The composition of this oil is recorded in Exodus 30:22–31—myrrh, cinnamon, calamus, cassia, with olive oil. I imagine the fragrance filled the air and was agreeable to every bystander.

In addition, it is like the dew of Hermon (v. 3). It is life-giving, encourages fruitfulness, and refreshes the souls of pilgrims wearied by the strife and malice of the world.

ii. The Possibility of the Partnership

As noted, this is not an appeal to unity at all costs. It is a call to unity among brethren. I am not arguing for an unbiblical ecumenism. The prayer of Christ, "that they may be one, as we are" (John 17:11) has nothing to do with Christians uniting with those in spiritual darkness. Nor are we to become doctrinal minimalists and dismiss the importance of convictions.

So, what is the basis of our unity? The picture given of Aaron the high priest ought to make us consider our great high priest, Jesus Christ. As Aaron was anointed, so Christ was anointed and filled with the Spirit without measure (John 3:34). And as the oil flowed from the priest's head to the body, so the Spirit of God flows from Christ to His Church. Thus, as the body only enjoys unity as it is in subjection to its head, so the Church only enjoys unity as it is in subjection to Christ. So how do we determine those that are in subjection to Christ?

Certainly there are truths so fundamental that a rejection of them puts one in a place of heterodoxy. The first century Church united in submission to the apostles' doctrine before they were ever in fellowship with one another (Acts 2:42). Doctrine comes before fellowship, just as a precise making of the oil came before the anointing. Truth matters, but there is a balance.

This balance can be seen in the godly Presbyterian minister, Robert Murray M'Cheyne. He writes,

> "I was once permitted to unite in celebrating the Lord's Supper in an upper room in Jerusalem. There were fourteen present, the most of whom, I had good reason to believe, knew and loved the Lord Jesus Christ. Several were godly Episcopalians, two were converted Jews, and one a Christian from Nazareth, converted under the American missionaries. The bread and wine were dispensed in the Episcopal manner, and most were kneeling as they received them."[21]

Many of us would choke in such a setting. But M'Cheyne did not allow his views and preferences to blind him to an acceptable adherence to the Lord's Table.

In the same article, he addresses the challenge of unity between Gospel ministers. He concludes,

> "where any minister of any denomination holds the Head, is sound in doctrine and blameless in life, preaches Christ and Him crucified as the only way of pardon, and the only source of holiness, especially if he has been owned of God in the conversion of souls and up-building of saints, we are bound to hold ministerial communion with him, whenever Providence opens the way. What are we that we should shut our pulpits against such a man?"[22]

This is the perspective of a God-fearing minister whose congregation the Spirit graced with revival. Learn from him.

iii. The Product of the Partnership

The Zion mentioned in this Psalm may not be Jerusalem. There is a Zion synonymous with Hermon (Deut. 4:48). But the point is that unity brings heaven's blessing to earth. That is what is signified in verse 3.

What is the blessing? The blessing of the covenant. The psalmist looked for more evidence of the Lord's promise to save and never forsake His people. And where will it happen? Where there is unity among brethren.

Does the blessing of God that advances Christ's kingdom matter to you? Are you willing to examine your thoughts of doctrinal superiority? Are you prepared to kill your prejudices?

Even good men can fall foul of sinful bigotry. Consider how the Erskine brothers turned on Whitefield:

> "The Erskines, upon hearing of the preaching of the Rev. George Whitefield, in England, invited him to Scotland, where he preached for Mr. Ralph Erskine, at Dunfermline. Proposals were now made to this great evangelical preacher, to join himself to the Associate Presbytery, which he rejected in the most peremptory manner. The conversation which took place between the parties, on this occasion, may be seen in 'Gillies' Life of Whitefield.' Immediately upon this refusal, the Seceders rejected him and his ministry, openly, and pursued him with as much bitterness of persecution."[23]

This is a blot on the Scottish ministers, but it is not unique to them. I fear the Judgment will reveal too much of this spirit in many churches. The apostolic exhortation is, "Finally, be ye all of one mind, having compassion one of another, love as brethren, be pitiful, be courteous: Not rendering evil for evil, or railing for railing: but contrariwise blessing; knowing that ye are thereunto called, that ye should inherit a blessing" (1 Pet. 3:8–9).

Do we not wish to inherit more blessing? Perfect unity is not necessary for revival; otherwise, it would be impossible. But if you want to be a spiritually revived Christian and to encourage others to seek the Lord with greater fervency, then you must pursue unity with your brethren. Pursue it, maintain it, and treasure it for the glory of God.

CHAPTER 7

The President of Revival

And the word of the LORD came unto Jonah the second time, saying, Arise, go unto Nineveh, that great city, and preach unto it the preaching that I bid thee

JONAH 3

By their very nature, genuine revivals are unusual. They do not happen all the time. And when they happen, they do not occur to the same extent for one simple reason: God is sovereign.

No biblical example evidences this more than Jonah's ministry to Nineveh. Nothing but a sovereign act of God can explain the spiritual awakening that takes place among the Ninevites.

Genesis 10:11 tells us that Nineveh was built by Asher, a grandson of Noah. It was one of the oldest cities in the world. By Jonah's time, it had also become one of the greatest cities of the world—sixty miles in circumference surrounded by walls. Jonah 4:11 tells us there were 120,000 children, giving an estimated population of around 700,000 people. A huge size for a city of antiquity.

Thus, it is not surprising that three times in Jonah, God describes Nineveh as a "great city" (Jonah 1:2; 3:2; 4:11). But as much as it was a great city in size, population, and significance, it was also a city of great sin (Jonah 1:2).

But even though there was such wickedness in that city, it was the location of one of the greatest revivals on record. And it happened, not in Israel, or Europe, or the Americas, but in modern day Iraq. Let this be a reminder to us that God is interested in working in every nation.

1. Revival Despite a Disadvantaged Place

Assyria was a heathen nation, and Nineveh was a heathen city. They had no God-appointed priesthood, God-inspired Word, or a history of God-sent prophets. They knew little or nothing of the promised Messiah, or pardon through the blood of God's Lamb.

Despite being a heathen place devoid of divine truth, God noted their living. Classical deism suggests God does not intervene in the affairs of men. From the prophecy of Jonah, evidently He does.

But what we must remember is that, without divine intervention, spiritual advantages can become a reason for greater judgment. Israel had everything Nineveh did not, and Jesus said to them, "The men of Nineveh shall rise in judgment with this generation, and shall condemn it: because they repented at the preaching of Jonas; and, behold, a greater than Jonas is here" (Matt. 12:41).

Israel had all the privileges. Later, they would have a greater prophet in their midst, the incarnate Son of God, but "His own received Him not" (John 1:11). Advantages only go so far. Unless the Lord acts, no society has hope.

ii. Revival Despite a Depraved People

Before we can understand the extent of this spiritual awakening, we must grasp how sinful Nineveh was.

Historically, the Assyrians were a cruel people. Much has been said about their cruelty, but we should be cautious about making generalizations. However, we know they were a people of warfare. Experts in torture, brutality, and laying siege against cities (such as the siege Sennacherib led some time after the ministry of Jonah). They pioneered having a professional national standing army. This is something we have become accustomed to, but Israel was forbidden, and was considered by some of the American Founding Fathers (perhaps surprisingly) as a danger to liberty.

In Jonah 1:2, the word "wickedness" is used in Genesis 6:5. "And God saw that the wickedness of man was great in the earth, and that every imagination of the thoughts of his heart was only evil continually."

This text gives the reason for the flood. The city of Nineveh is similar, and their sin had "come up before me," i.e. it is rising before God's face. It is a description of its increasing intensity and development. The Ninevites were getting worse. This language is sometimes used in relation to offering up sacrifices to God. Instead of offering sacrifices, the Ninevites were offering their sin to God.

So, were they likely to repent? With warnings of impending judgment, we might have expected a response like Lot's sons-in-law (Gen. 19:14). Man by nature is depraved. Jonathan Edwards is often quoted as saying, "You contribute nothing to your salvation except the sin that made it necessary." Any thought that men inherently seek after God flies in the face of Romans 3:10–12. Our expectation, then, is that they will run Jonah out of the city. The surprise is that an entire city of hostile, savage pagans turn to God (v. 5).

How is this possible? There is no way to explain this repentance except by recognizing it as a sovereign act of God. Even the king comes under conviction. Think of the worst city in your nation. Now imagine preaching in it and seeing such a response to the preaching of God's Word. It is utterly astounding.

It should not discourage us that such an outpouring of the Spirit is ultimately out of our control. If revival was not a sovereign act of God, then prayer would be a waste of time. We pray because God alone can turn the hearts of men. Thus, we keep praying in expectation. G. Campbell Morgan said, "We cannot organize revival, but we can set our sails to catch the wind from Heaven when God chooses to blow upon His people once again."[24]

III. Revival Despite a Deficient Preacher

In every revival, God uses means. Often we make a big deal about the men He uses. But human instrumentality is not inherently essential; **it is divinely ordained.** This distinction is important to recognize. God does not need us, but has chosen to appoint men to bring His Word (Acts 11:13–15; Rom. 10:14).

Even so, the preacher is not the presiding factor in revival. In one of the greatest moves of the Spirit of God, the Lord shows the deficiencies of the preacher.

First, *he cannot go* (Jonah 1:1–3; 3:1–3). Whatever grace was in Jonah's heart was not sufficient to prompt obedience in him. So God sends him a message in the form of difficult circumstances. The voice of providence lays him low and puts him in the belly of a whale. God gives Jonah something He would not promise to the Ninevites; namely, a second chance.

While God never winds the clock back for us, He does give us new beginnings. God loves to give His people new beginnings. But these only commence when we die. And I do not mean physical death, but a deep mortification of self. God fashioned the circumstances in Jonah's life to bring him to such a death-like experience.

My friend, we need this. Jesus said, "If any man will come after me, let him deny himself, and take up his cross daily, and follow me" (Luke 9:23). When He spoke these words, taking up the cross meant death. Too many of us protect our carefree lives. We guard that which needs to die in us. Octavius Winslow observed,

> "Beloved reader, in thy heart and in mine, the principle of this sin exists; and who can search it out, and root it out, but the Lord the Spirit? 'If we through the Spirit mortify the deeds of

the body, we shall live.' Is thy covenant God and Father dealing with thee now? Pray that this may be one blessed result, *the abasement of self within thee*, the discovering of it to thee in all its modifications and deformity, and its entire subjection to the cross of Jesus. Blessed pruning, if the tendency and the effect are, to lay thee in the dust before the Lord, to cause thee to loathe thyself, and to go softly and lowlily all thy days!"[25]

We need to be intentional in taking stock of where we really are. Although our mind must dwell much more on Christ than on our own corruption, a deep awareness of our nature is an aid to appreciating our Lord Jesus and serving Him. Have you died to everything holding you back from being as useful to God as you might be?

While evil men will run without being sent, good men need the Lord's sustaining grace to serve faithfully and powerfully. Die to self and He will provide it.

Second, *he cannot speak* (Jonah 3:2, 4). God reveals to Jonah what is to come and tells him what to say. No doubt this is an abbreviated version of the message. But the point is the preacher has nothing to say except what God bids him to say. That is his job. God does not ask preachers to be witty, but to be faithful. Just give forth His Word.

What happens? "The people of Nineveh believed God" (v. 5). It is not Jonah they believe, it is God. In a day of personality cults and celebrity preachers capitalizing on biblical illiteracy, this is refreshing. People must heed the Word of God, not the word of man.

Third, *he cannot save* (Jonah 2:9). Jonah learned by personal experience that salvation is the prerogative of God alone. In fact, God's sovereignty in salvation bothered Jonah. Jonah ran away from the call to Nineveh because he knew God intended to call them to repentance and He did not want that (Jonah 4:2).

As an aside, the reference to God repenting does not indicate God changing His mind. God cannot change for the better, and will not change for the worse (Mal. 3:6). Since God stays the same, it is the people who change. God sent Nineveh the right message to effect change in them (Jer. 18:7–8).

Since we know Assyria laid siege to Jerusalem a few decades later, the awakening was temporary. Lives were changed, but much of the culture remained. This is a reminder of the importance of revival *and* reformation. To leave a lasting legacy, we must reform all aspects of our communities to the Word of God. This is how we serve our generation (Acts 13:36).

Are you serving your generation as an instrument in the hand of God? The task may seem too great. Jonah had a gargantuan task. Called to preach to a foreign culture, in a vast city, with a short time-frame. Nineveh was not a favorable place for revival to occur. Nor were the people or even the preacher ideal from a human perspective.

Yet, there was a revival. Martyn Lloyd-Jones said that revival is "a passing by of God's glory."[26] That is true. It is something we have no control over. But nations have been upended by less than perfect preachers who simply obeyed God and preached the Word.

John Knox was such a man. He had a vision to turn his beloved nation of Scotland into something akin to John Calvin's Geneva. This vision was realized in the removal of the false gospel of popery, and filling the land with faithful, Bible preaching churches. It would be untrue to say it was a clean and simple process. But Knox, by his leadership and especially his preaching, transformed Scotland. Iain Murray sums it up well, "The only true explanation of Knox's preaching is in words he applied to others of his fellow countrymen, 'God gave his Holy Spirit to simple men in great abundance.'"[27]

Are you a simple man? It is not more learning you need. It is more of God. And the only place to get that is to go to God Himself and plead for His Spirit.

CHAPTER 8

The Patience in Revival

These all continued with one accord in prayer and supplication, with the women, and Mary the mother of Jesus, and with his brethren.

Acts 1:14

In 1892, as a young man in his twenties, John Nelson Hyde left his home in America to travel to India. He believed that God had called him to preach the Gospel in the Punjab region.

As he began his journey, he read a letter from a friend that said, "I shall not cease praying for you, dear John, until you are filled with the Holy Spirit."[28]

With pride governing his heart, the young missionary found himself annoyed. The comment implied something was lacking in his life. After struggling over it for a time, he humbled himself and recorded, "I would do anything and be anything, but the Holy Spirit I would have at any cost."[29]

But the mere acknowledgement of his need was only the first step. After about eight years of barrenness and struggle, he began to seek God in earnest. Over the next five years, God continued to deepen Hyde's experience in prayer. He often wrestled with God for hours. On one occasion in 1904, Hyde and a friend spent 30 days in prayer.[30] God was working in his life.

Hyde, along with friends, formed the Punjab Prayer Union. They aimed to set aside 30 minutes every day to pray for revival.

At the Sialkot Convention of 1905, God came down. At the close of the first service, the entire congregation fell to their knees and prayed until dawn. The power of the Spirit was evident, and we are told that the effect was felt throughout all India. Hundreds and hundreds were being converted, and missionary zeal was aflame. But it began with the burden of one man, 'Praying Hyde.'

John Hyde labored patiently and saw God work. At the age of 46, having touched the lives of countless thousands of people, God was pleased to remove Hyde from this world.

So we ask, is revival a sovereign work of a sovereign God? Yes. But do we have a responsibility to seek God earnestly? Perhaps more than we like to admit. And our problem is that we lack the patience to wait on God.

1. The Conformity of Those Waiting

While a fear of the Jews was real among the followers of Christ, the disciples did not allow it to keep them from their duty. The Lord had given them instructions, and it was important that they conformed to His will (Luke 24:49; Acts 1:4).

Whatever personal plans they had were shelved. They dropped everything to pray. Christ had given them a much higher calling. Namely, to wait for the promise of the Father. So what did they do (Acts 1:12–14)?

We learn that they "abode" i.e. tarried. They did what Christ told them to do. How refreshing. We live in a day where men are obsessed with their destiny to the neglect of their duty. We have a high view of destiny and a low view of duty because we have a high view of self and a low view of service.

"Hath the Lord as great delight in burnt offerings and sacrifices, as in obeying the voice of the Lord? Behold, to obey is better than sacrifice, and to hearken than the fat of rams" (1 Sam. 15:22). See also Eccl. 12:13–14; Luke 11:28.

If only we would learn from John Bunyan, "What God says is best, is indeed best, though all the men in the world are against it."[31]

Instead of obeying God and waiting in prayer, we reinvent the Church. The Church looks different than it did generations ago, not because of *obedience* but because of *convenience*.

Why have our pulpits weakened in their warnings against sin? Why have churches abandoned prayer meetings? Why is there a resurgence of architectural and liturgical aesthetics? The greatest advances of the Church have not needed an emphasis on such things.

We are compromised and spiritually impoverished. The changes in the Church are not out of devotion to the truth, but show our love of ease, our willingness to compromise, and our satisfaction with a form of casual Christianity. There is no cross. No suffering. No blood, sweat, or tears. We have dulled the sharp edge of Christ's call to take up the cross daily and follow Him (Luke 9:23; 14:27). We will follow Him in the consoling themes of forgiveness, but we will not follow Him in the garden to pray. Where are the *all on the altar* Christians (Rom. 12:1–2)?

Christ said, "Tarry in Jerusalem," and the apostles went straight to Jerusalem to pray, even though it was the most dangerous place on earth for them at that time.

11. The Company of Those Waiting

If you read the life of John Hyde, you learn that he placed an emphasis on united prayer. He learned this from the apostles. Consider Acts 1:14.

First, they were *an experienced company.* "These all continued…" i.e. the apostles. The men taught by Christ. They were the most experienced in the assembly. It was their instruction that new believers would follow (Acts 2:42). Being in the presence of mature believers is a great blessing. Prayer meetings are helped by the presence of Christians who have learned what it is to lay hold upon God. We darken our hope for the future when we keep God's people away from the example of older, battled-hardened saints who know how to pray. Children want everything instantly, but patience comes by experience. This is why an infantile Church will never see revival.

Second, they were *an equal company*. "With the women and Mary" i.e. the women were there to pray. By using the term "equal," I do not mean to espouse egalitarianism. But while I reject women holding office in the Church, I do not believe we must exclude them from public participation in prayer. Some good brethren oppose women praying in prayer meetings, citing 1 Timothy 2 in their defense. But there is a distinction between corporate worship services and prayer meetings. This distinction opens up the right for women to pray with men. The preposition of this text infers that the women were praying as well. Perhaps the prayers were silent, but I will differ here with those that believe so. A woman with her head covered (1 Cor. 11:5) does not need to be viewed as usurping authority over men when she prays. The public prayers of women, even in the presence of men, are not ignored by Christ. He loves to hear from them (Matt. 15:22–28).

Third, they were *an expanding company.* "His brethren" i.e. Christ's half brothers. When we examine the biblical evidence, we can determine that they are new converts (John 7:5). And new converts should be taught the importance of prayer and encouraged to gather for prayer. It is instructive for them, and despite their limitations, they should be allowed to join in. Few sounds are sweeter to hear than the prayers of a new believer. It is tragic that many Christians never hear it because they have no prayer meeting or there are no new converts.

III. The Continuity of Those Waiting

If ever there was a blueprint for the Church's prayer life, it is in the book of Acts. There are indications of prayer in almost every chapter.

Should someone question the legitimacy of prayer meetings, we need not look any further than the book of Acts (Acts 1:14; 4:23–31; 12:5; 12:12). With such explicit practice, can a church be called a New Testament church when it never has a prayer meeting? And can we be considered serious Christians if we neglect prayer meetings? Note Acts 1:14 carefully, "These all continued with one accord in prayer and supplication, with the women, and Mary the mother of Jesus, and with his brethren."

First, *there was faithfulness in their continuity*. They "continued," i.e. they were steadfast. They displayed perseverance. For several days they waited on God.

Why are we reluctant to wait on God like this? Even when we do pray, we are more like the disciples in the garden of Gethsemane, suffering under the weakness of the flesh. What made the difference in the apostles between Gethsemane and the Upper Room? The resurrection. A view of the risen Christ will give birth to persevering prayer. There is a weakness in us because we do not live consciously in the reality of a risen Savior. Therefore, often there is a correlation between faithless prayer and lifeless spiritual affections.

Second, *there was fervency in their continuity*. Their activity is described as "prayer and supplication." Terms are multiplied to reflect the fervency of prayer. This was not a prayer meeting for the sake of a prayer meeting. This was a meeting with God. And they had the promise of the Spirit that they brought before the Lord.

The most effective kind of prayer is that which is built upon a promise from God, such as the promise of the Holy Spirit. We are much more patient when we are waiting for something than when we are waiting for nothing, especially when what we are waiting for is something we value.

The key, then, is to have promises from God and to value them. The Bible is full of them, and they need to burn into your heart and flood into your prayers with hope and expectation. To keep coming with "Lord, you said…" "Lord, you said…" "Lord, you said…" Too many of our prayer meetings are taken up with temporal matters in the lives of saints, while the unregenerate traversing a path to hell are left unnamed before the throne of grace. May God teach us what it is to be burdened, especially for matters of eternal consequence.

Third, *there was fellowship in their continuity*. They "continued with one accord," i.e. in harmony. Biblical fellowship has little to do with having common interests in employment, hobbies, and our status of life. What united everyone was their vision of a crucified, risen, and ascended Christ (Acts 1:3). This was the basis of their unity and the foundation of their confidence in prayer. They believed in the victory of Christ's work and had seen Him ascend into heaven with His hands outstretched to bless them (Luke 24:50–51). They knew He was reigning in victory from His throne (Acts 2:33–36).

Your work, dear Christian, is to wait on God for His power. There will be no personal or corporate revival if we are not seeking the face of God.

When John Hyde started the Punjab Prayer Union, he challenged participants with these questions. Consider them soberly.

> "Are you praying for quickening in your own life, in the life of your fellow workers, and in the Church? Are you longing for greater power of the Holy Spirit in your own life and work, and are you convinced that you cannot go on without this power? Will you pray that you may not be ashamed of Jesus? Do you believe that prayer is the great means for securing this spiritual awakening? Will you set apart one half hour each day as soon as possible to pray for this awakening, and are you willing to pray till the awakening comes?"[32]

Arguably, it is the last few words we find most difficult. It is easy to experience and express temporary zeal for divine matters, but do we have the patience to "pray till the awakening comes?" The first century believers did, and every so often God raises a few people to follow in their footsteps. Will you be one of them?

CHAPTER 9

The Product of Revival

Now when they heard this, they were pricked in their heart, and said unto Peter and to the rest of the apostles, Men and brethren, what shall we do?

Acts 2:37-47

When we think of revival, the day of Pentecost is often the first scene that comes to mind. A handful of believers waiting in prayer turns into thousands in a matter of hours.

What excites us in reading Acts 2 is the suddenness of the display of divine power. Out of nowhere, it seems, multitudes were awakened. We are told, "Now when they heard this, they were pricked in their heart" (Acts 2:37). The word "pricked" has the idea of being stung to the quick, or being pierced through.

This pricking is what we call conviction. Conviction is a common mark in every outpouring of the Spirit and results in widespread evidence of regeneration. Regeneration is the biblical doctrine whereby sinners do not merely mentally assent to the truth, but experience a change of heart by the power of the Holy Ghost. This distinction is always emphasized in revival.

George Whitefield, the great English evangelist, often faced opposition for insisting that regeneration was the foundation of spiritual life. But he kept preaching it (some suggest he preached on the new birth over three thousand times). As a result, he was an instrument in awakenings that read like Acts 2.

However, the vast majority of revivals do not commence with an objective to see thousands converted. The concern is sin in the Church and a desire to recover the presence of God. But when sin is dealt with and God's presence is known, often it results in a spiritual harvest like Pentecost.

So what should we expect if a revival—similar to Acts 2—happened today?

1. The Increase of the Church

Every revival results in an increase of the Church. When God comes upon His Church in power, the consequence is not only revived saints, but new converts.

This is what happened at Pentecost. Peter did not preach the greatness of man. As Ian Paisley once said, he was not engaged in the business of "corpse washing," i.e. trying to improve the appearance of sinners dead in their sin. He was in the resurrection business. He called the crowds to "repent."

In one day, God dramatically multiplied His Church (Acts 2:41). From about 120 disciples meeting for prayer in the Upper Room (Acts 1:15) to three thousand genuine converts in one day! Christ does not sit idle at the right hand of the Majesty on high (Heb. 1:3). He is actively extending His kingdom through the preaching of the Gospel (Ps. 110:1).

Church history also shows us that large increases can happen suddenly. The Kirk o' Shotts revival of 1630 in Scotland is one such event. After a communion season, John Livingstone addressed a large congregation in the churchyard. According to his own testimony, he preached "with such liberty and melting of heart, as I never had the like in public all my life-time."[33] Eyewitness accounts suggest up to five hundred were visibly affected.

Over and above localized awakenings, revival can transform nations in a generation. A recent example of this is South Korea. In 50 years (1945–1995), the country went from an estimated 2% to 26% Christian population.[34] The vast majority of the growth has been Protestant and Presbyterian.

At this very moment, there are encouraging signs of significant Gospel advance in Iran.[35] Christ has not stopped extending His kingdom.

Do our hearts not yearn for something like this? Yes, the increase belongs to God. But our prayer meetings—if we have them at all—seem devoid of an earnest desire for His kingdom to come (Luke 11:2).

ii. The Interests of the Church

Jonathan Edwards considered it vital to raise the affections of his hearers to God through the truth. He argued, "I should think myself in the way of my duty to raise the affections of my hearers as high as possibly I can, provided that they are affected with nothing but truth, and with affections that are not disagreeable to the nature of the subject."[36]

Today, the aim for much of the American Church is lower. There appears to be no shame in churches gathering on Sundays to watch the World Cup Final or the Super Bowl. No one bats an eyelid when July Fourth or Christmas Day coincides with the Lord's Day and worship services get moved or canceled. How is this justifiable? What were the first century believers interested in?

First, *there was a love for the Scriptures.* Over half of the verses of Peter's sermon are from the Old Testament. When God saved three thousand souls on the day of Pentecost, it was "when they heard this" (v. 37), and when they "gladly received his word" (v. 41).

We are then told that they "continued steadfastly in the apostle's doctrine" (v. 42). They could not get enough. They craved the Scriptures. And their faith is underlined when the Spirit says they "believed" (v. 44).

Do not forget that these were people already familiar with the Old Testament Scriptures. But they enjoyed a newfound love and hunger for it when they saw Jesus Christ as the subject of every Old Testament book.

Our churches need more Bible, not less. And they need to see more of Jesus in the Bible, not less.

Second, *there was a love for the saints* as they gave themselves to "fellowship and breaking of bread" (v. 42). People were not coerced to do this. Sanctified conversation was normal, and there was a desire to spend time with one another.

Of course, this also means that everyone must be willing to restore broken relationships and obey Jesus when He said, "Therefore if thou bring thy gift to the altar, and there rememberest that thy brother hath ought against thee; Leave there thy gift before the altar, and go thy way; first be reconciled to thy brother, and then come and offer thy gift" (Matt. 5:24–25).

Third, *there was a love for supplication*, or "prayers" (v. 42). This has been more fully expounded in the preceding chapters, but suffice to say that in revival, personal prayer and corporate prayer are central to the Christian's daily life.

Thus, we have a litmus test for our spirituality. If we do not possess love for the Scriptures, saints, and supplication, we have a spiritual malady. All this pleases God, and we should not wait for revival before we endeavor to live this way. We should exhibit an interest in such spiritual activity throughout our lives.

III. The Impact of the Church

What is the result of this revival? Aside from the conversions, "fear came upon every soul" (v. 43). This is a common component in revival (Acts 5:11; 19:17).

Do you not desire God to come to your community in such a way where men can no longer ignore Him?

In 1622, the aged and esteemed Scottish preacher, Robert Bruce, was banished on two occasions to

Inverness—a small and ungodly town. Nothing happened during his first banishment. But things were different the second time. By the preaching of one man, God turned the entire community on its head. Souls were saved, while prayer and fellowship meetings were maintained every evening.[37] Independent preacher James Haldane (1768–1851) remarked on the evidence of Bruce's lingering influence even at the turn of the century.[38]

As we witness all the unbiblical ideologies of our day, our tendency is to blame outside forces. But "judgment must begin at the house of God" (1 Pet. 4:17).

Alan Cairns used to share an experience he had when he first met Jordan Khan. Khan, a preacher from India, had been influenced by John "Praying" Hyde. In 1962, Khan visited Northern Ireland. His English was slow and broken. But when he prayed, heaven opened and everyone was brought into—what felt like—a face-to-face encounter with God. Here was a man who spent hours every day in prayer. Cairns remarked that when you prayed with Jordan Khan, you went to places in prayer you never knew existed. He stated many times, "That night changed my ministry."

It is said that if Khan ever heard someone question whether Pentecost was for today, he would glare at them and ask, "Have you spent 10 days in prayer seeking for the Holy Spirit?"

Brothers and sisters, it is not the sound of wind or the appearance of tongues of fire we look for. It is for the outpouring of the Spirit in power, sent in answer to believing prayer. Will you not pray for it? Will you not wait for it?

When the evangelist, Brownlow North, addressed the Free Church of Scotland General Assembly in 1859, he rebuked them for their "neglect of united prayer—the appointed means of bringing down the Holy Spirit." He went on to say:

> "I say it, because I believe it, that the Scotch, with all their morality, so called, and their outward decency, respectability, and love of preaching, are not a praying people. Take the Presbyterian Churches,—I am not speaking of the Free Church, the Established Church, or any other Church—take the Churches of the land, and you find congregations of from 1,400 to 1,600 on Sabbaths, and at the prayer meetings on Tuesdays you find thirty, forty, fifty, and sixty people. Sirs, is not this the truth? The neglect of prayer proves, to my mind, that there is a large amount of *practical infidelity*. If people believed that there was a real, existing, personal God, they would ask Him for what they wanted, and they would get what they asked. But they do not ask, because they do not believe or expect to receive. Why do I say this? Because I want to get Christians to remember, that though preaching is one of the great means appointed by God for the conversion of sinners, yet, unless God give the increase, Paul may plant and Apollos may

water in vain; and God says He will be inquired of. O Ministers! excuse me—you gave me this chance of speaking—urge upon your people to come to the prayer meeting. O Christians, go more to more prayer meetings than you do. And when you go to the prayer meeting, try and realise more that there is *use in prayer*."[39]

Dear Christian, if you wish to see another effusion of the Spirit in your day, you must gather with other believers for prayer.

CHAPTER 10

The Praise of Revival

*And Saul was consenting unto his death.
And at that time there was a great persecution against
the church which was at Jerusalem; and they were all
scattered abroad throughout the regions of Judaea and
Samaria, except the apostles.*

Acts 8:1-12

When God sends revival, such is the breath of God into the lives of believers that things cannot stay the same. How you study, how you work, how you relate to family, how you engage in church, how you think about your future, etc, it all changes.

Everything changes.

And it changes because we discover that there is an unparalleled joy when God visits His people. "When the Lord turned again the captivity of Zion, we were like them that dream. Then was our mouth filled with laughter, and our tongue with singing: then said they among the heathen, The Lord hath done great things for them. The Lord hath done great things for us; whereof we are glad" (Ps. 126:1–3).

And so it was in Samaria where we read in Acts 8:8, "And there was great joy in that city."

1. The Means of Revival Praise

How does God bring joy to this city?

First, there is *the man*. Philip first appears as a deacon where he is described as a man of "honest report, full of the Holy Ghost and wisdom" (Acts 6:3). This was a man with a consistent testimony of Christian living before the world, with evidence of the Spirit's work in his life. He was also known to be wise. Here was a man who was placed in an office of the church because he was already living a life that was committed to Christ and His people.

When his friend Stephen was martyred, Philip did not step back from ministry in fear for his life. Why did Philip leave Jerusalem and go to Samaria? Was he afraid? Hardly. It is more likely that the apostles sent him from Jerusalem.

As we learn from Christ, "He that is faithful in that which is least is faithful also in much" (Luke 16:10). Philip had been a faithful deacon, and the apostles commissioned him as one of the first missionaries during the persecution.

Second, there is *the message*. We already saw that Christ is the subject of Peter's preaching in Acts 2. The same is true in Acts 3. When the miraculous healing of the lame man at the temple occurred, it opened a door to preach Christ. When Stephen was arrested, he preached Christ. When Peter was sent to Cornelius, it was to preach Christ. When Paul moved from city to city, it was to preach Christ. And so it was for Philip (Acts 8:5, 12).

Christian, demand that your preacher preach Christ. Repackaging topical self-help talks with Christian terminology is not preaching Christ. Goats love it. But sheep respond to the voice of the Shepherd, and it is the only message God blesses in revival.

ii. The Need for Revival Praise

If we recall what happened in John 4, we can assume there were some believers in Samaria. However, it was still a place of great need. The Gospel brought a contrast of atmosphere in Samaria, summarized in Acts 8:8, "And there was great joy in that city."

Not that Samaria was in a state of abnormal misery. It was probably just like any other place. The lack of spiritual joy continued undetected and many of the people were living under spiritual oppression because of the sorcery of Simon (Acts 8:9–11).

Nothing has changed in our own day. Simon was a local celebrity. He is a picture of the 21st century entertainment and social media industry. People are spellbound by it. They love it. They think it brings them joy. But in reality, they are falling infinitely short of the joy of experiencing the risen Christ.

Many today are living their life behind a filter. God's intention for man to enjoy meaningful relationships has been replaced by a digital counterfeit. A good relationship is now defined by likes and comments on your social media posts.

God's grand purpose for our lives has been reduced to a life-goal of gaining more followers to our feed, subscribers to our channel, or achievements on the latest video game.

We are living under a spell. And this spell robs from you the ability to appreciate what matters, and creates an insatiable appetite for the meaningless.

Arguably, the greatest casualty of this is the youth. But that is also where the Church today has its greatest hope. God loves to remove the scales of sorcery from each new generation.

Solomon Stoddard, grandfather of Jonathan Edwards, testified to—what he called—five harvests during his ministry.[40] These were definite spiritual awakenings in his community. In each of them, the most affected demographic was the young people.

The history of revivals will show this to be the case over and over again.

When I see young people taken up with the trifles of the world, I cannot help but feel it has deceived them. Their nature craves a regular dopamine hit, and the spell of modern entertainment along with the illusion of social acceptance meets that natural yearning.

But they are missing the mark completely. Many modern past-times function as a kind of placebo. A counterfeit. God made man for higher attainments than to satisfy his physiological needs with habits of no consequence.

This is where revival comes in. It awakens people to the ways the world has bewitched them, and shows them what they really need—namely, God Himself.

III. The Exclusivity of Revival Praise

What will our future be like? Some imagine it to be as George Orwell depicted in his book *Nineteen Eighty-Four,* where we cannot do what we want. Others argue it is more accurately portrayed by Aldous Huxley in *Brave New World*. In this future, we are encouraged to do what we want to keep us from doing what is right.

Huxley wrote to Orwell in 1949 and said,

> "Within the next generation I believe that the world's rulers will discover that infant conditioning and narco-hypnosis are more efficient, as instruments of government, than clubs and prisons, and that the lust for power can be just as completely satisfied by suggesting people into loving their servitude as by flogging and kicking them into obedience."[41]

The truth is, it is all slavery. Though it functions in varying degrees, the outcome is a form of bondage.

What is the only and exclusive answer? The joy of the Gospel of Christ poured forth in power. Yet, we must remember that not every ministry effort by the Early Church resulted in the outcome witnessed in Samaria. Every preacher has to accept that while one may sow and another water, it is only God that gives the increase. But we must look for brighter days.

Our world has made us consumers of joy instead of habitations of joy. Christ, who is joy incarnate, does not live in the hearts of men.

When our joy depends on what we can buy with money, it is because we do not have access to the source of all joy.

Spiritual revival is the recovery of genuine joy. Consider what happened under the ministry of Jonathan Edwards in Northampton, MA. Edwards recorded in 1735,

> "the town seemed to be full of the presence of God. It never was so full of love, nor of joy, and yet so full of distress, as it was then. There were remarkable tokens of God's presence in almost every house. It was a time of joy in families, on account of salvation being brought unto them; parents rejoicing over their children as new born, and husbands over their wives, and wives over their husbands…"[42]

They experienced Acts 8:8, "there was great joy in that city."

My friend, we are richer than ever, yet poorer. We are healthier than ever, yet sicker and more medicated. What is wrong with us? The fullness of God's power has departed, and so we are left to find satisfaction in carnal charms and charismatic personalities.

It is recorded concerning the 1858 revival in New York City:

> "In this revival, some of the worst of men have been made the subjects of renewing grace. They have been the subjects of special and earnest prayer. And instead of giving them up, and considering them as 'devoted to destruction', as has been formerly the fact in regard to such cases, there has been a rejoicing confidence and expectation that God would glorify the exceeding riches of his grace, in bringing these men to repentance… The time has come when the people of God have been made to believe, not theoretically but practically, that nothing is too hard for the Lord."[43]

It is true. Nothing is too hard for the Lord. May God help us to see our enslavement and to cry out in earnest for another revival, that it may be said in our communities that there is "great joy."

Perhaps you, yes you, reading this book, will do what the rest of us have been too carnal and spiritually indolent to do. You will remove every known sin, every known compromise, and every lesser ambition from your life and seek God for another revival.

Section II:
Sermons on Prayer

This section contains a selection of sermons on the topic of Prayer preached at various conferences.

CHAPTER 11

An Earnest Call to Follow Good Men

That thou mayest walk in the way of good men, and keep the paths of the righteous.

PROVERBS 2:20

When some come to understand the free grace of God which is in Christ, they appear to think it means the removal of all personal responsibility.

These professing Christians refuse strong exhortations to exercise themselves in precise matters of holiness because Christ is the believer's righteousness. And this reaches into their prayer lives as well. They imagine that we no longer need to give ourselves to prayer because Christ is our intercessor.

Such thinking flies in the face of John's words, "He that saith he abideth in him ought himself also so to walk, even as he walked" (1 John 2:6).

We are to give ourselves to following Christ's example—it is the chief calling of our lives. But since we do not have the incarnate Christ before us, the call to follow the example of good men is broadened in Scripture.

1. The Biblical Evidence to Follow Good Men

You are no doubt aware "there is not a just man upon earth, that doeth good, and sinneth not" (Eccl. 7:20). While the doctrine of man's depravity may be easy for the Calvinist to accept, we must also remember that grace makes men good.

We are told explicitly that Barnabas "was a good man, and full of the Holy Ghost and of faith" (Acts 11:24). Why had he become a good man? Because he, like you and me, was "created in Christ Jesus unto good works" (Eph. 2:10).

God glorifies Himself in transforming sinners. He works on us as a man might cut and polish a diamond in order to maximize its beauty and value.

But God also gives us that same desire to shine brightly for Him and to "work out your own salvation with fear and trembling" (Phil. 2:12). One way God aids us in achieving the goal of being good men is by giving us examples and calling us to follow them (1 Cor. 4:16; 11:1; Phil. 3:17; 2 Thess. 3:7)

Matthew Henry said, "There is a way which is peculiarly the way of good men, the way in which good men, as such, and as far as they have really been such, have always walked. It will be our wisdom to walk in that way."[44]

In other words, we do not have to reinvent how to live the Christian life. Success leaves a trail. Just find the strongest believers and shadow them. What follows is an attempt to help you find the trail you should be on.

II. The Biographical Examples of Good Men

I begin with David Brainerd, missionary to the Native Americans. Though he died at 29 years of age, Brainerd exemplified this need to follow good men. We read of him, "Sometime in April, 1738, I went to Mr. Fiske's, and lived with him during his life. I remember he advised me wholly to abandon young company, and associate myself with grave elderly people: which counsel I followed."[45]

Note the advice. Paul exhorts that all men, including young men, are to be "sober" (Tit. 2:2, 6). To understand how to glorify God in maturity, one must have a sense of gravity. Mr. Fiske believed the company of older men would help cultivate such graces in Brainerd, and Brainerd believed his advice was worth following.

What kind of man was David Brainerd? At 24 years of age, here is what we read in his diary:

> April 25 — "This morning I spent about two hours in secret duties, and was enabled more than ordinarily to agonize for immortal souls; though it was early in the morning, the sun scarcely shined at all, yet my body was quite wet with sweat."

April 27 — "O that my soul might never offer any dead, cold services to my God!"

April 28 — "I withdrew to my usual place of retirement in great peace and tranquility, spent about two hours in secret duties… God was so precious to my soul, that the world with all its enjoyments was infinitely vile. I had no more value for the favour of men, than for pebbles."

This is how his diary continues, in constant expressions of his hungering for God and lamentation over his sins. Note the proximity of the following dates:

June 13 — "I was in such an agony, from sun half an hour high, till near dark, that I was all over wet with sweat; but yet it seemed to me that I wasted away the day, and had done nothing. Oh my dear Jesus did sweat blood for poor souls! I longed for more compassion towards them."

June 18 — "I set apart this day for prayer to God, and spent most of the day in that duty."

June 19 — "Spent much time alone. My soul longed to be holy, and reached after God."

June 22 — "In the morning spent about two hours in prayer and meditation, with considerable delight."

June 30 — "Spent this day alone in the woods, in fasting and prayer."[46]

How would your diary look at 24 years of age? Is there not something here for us to follow? Does his devotion not resonate?

Too many of us are caught up in worldly matters more than is justifiable. We refuse to take seriously the words of Paul, "No man that warreth entangleth himself with the affairs of this life; that he may please him who hath chosen him to be a soldier" (2 Tim. 2:4).

But other men—men we should follow—achieved greater victory over the temptations of the world. In a letter written in 1740, a young George Whitefield said,

> "There is nothing I dread more than having my heart drawn away with earthly objects. When that time comes, it will be over with me indeed; I must then bid adieu to zeal and fervency of spirit, and in effect, bid the Lord Jesus to depart from me. For alas, what room can there be for God, when a rival hath taken possession of the heart?"[47]

There are endless examples of Christians that challenge us to live better. Examples that stretch us. These believers put a completely different light on life. But truth be told, we are better at talking about these men than we are following them. Will you be different?

III. The Blunt Exhortations From Good Men

Those of us living in the West have a rich heritage of godly examples to learn from and follow. Their exploits and exhortations fill our history books.

The Scottish Reformer, John Knox, understood that when the Church faces difficulty, the Christian's duty is to visit God. This comes out in the only sermon we have from him, which he wrote from memory after he preached it on August 19, 1565. He said,

> "Let us now humble ourselves in the presence of our God, and from the bottom of our hearts let us desire him to assist us with the power of his Holy Spirit… that albeit we see his church so diminished, that it appears to be brought, as it were, to utter extermination, we may be assured, that in our God there is great power and will, to increase the number of his chosen, until they are enlarged to the uttermost parts of the earth. Give us, O Lord! hearts to visit thee in time of affliction."[48]

The secret of these men was not in their natural gifts, but their diligence in prayer. However, when you look at many Reformed preachers today, you would think their sole duty was to preach the truth. If that is the case, the day will come when we can replace them with robots parroting sermons created with Artificial Intelligence.

For some Christians living today, that would be enough. But truth proclaimed without divine unction would not satisfy our Reformed forefathers. On one occasion, when a young preacher named Robert Blair was preaching, he had the eminent Robert Bruce in attendance. After the sermon, the young Blair approached Bruce to get his opinion. Bruce is said to have replied, "I found your sermon very polished and digested, but there is one thing I did miss in it—the Spirit of God, I found not that."[49]

Ouch! What would he say of the dusty sermons of today? Sermons that are far too often devoid of any heavenly influences.

As far short as we fall, this is not a time for quitting. This is a time to find and follow good men. Spurgeon was not afraid to elevate his hearers to a sense of higher duty. He said,

> "We never do anything in this world until we set our faces thoroughly to it. The warriors who win battles are those who are resolved to conquer or die. The heroes who emancipate nations are those who count no hazards and reckon no odds, but are resolved that the yoke shall be broken from the neck of their country. The merchants who prosper in this world are those who do their business with all their hearts, and watch for wealth with eagerness. The half-hearted man is nowhere in the race of life."[50]

This is not a time for half-heartedness. Listen to Whitefield again. At 52 years of age, and with just 4 years left to live, George Whitefield lamented over how little he had done and suffered for Christ, and resolved, "I will begin to begin to be a Christian."[51]

That is God's call to you, my friend—begin again.

Our problem is not a lack of desire, but a lack of perseverance in desire. But God can supply both the desire and the will to obey. Seek Him for it now.

CHAPTER 12

Blessed Retirements: The Life of James Calder

Man's record of man is always flawed to a greater or lesser degree. We do not know what God knows. And nowhere is man more likely to make a flawed judgment on another man than in judging his prayer life.

Despite this, examples can be helpful. Many come to mind—George Whitefield, David Brainerd, John Hyde, George Müller—all of them have been helpful to the wider Church.

But I wish to enlighten you on a lesser known Scottish minister, James Calder.[52] He referred to extended seasons of prayer as "blessed retirements." The term is not unique to him, but he seemed to be more inclined to use it than others when describing the discipline of shutting yourself away from the world to get alone with God.

1. Early Life

The son of a Presbyterian minister, James Calder, was born in 1712. We have no record of any conversion experience. Yet, from his earliest writings, it is plain that he was well-grounded in the Scriptures.

At 23 years of age, five years before his ordination, his diary contains a lamentation over the state of his heart a few days before the Lord's Supper:

> "Scarcely did I resolve to be a partaker, and in consequence thereof to essay some preparation of soul, when corruption sallied forth furiously upon me, and made great efforts to suppress these thoughts and resolutions; lust and corruptions haling one way, a sense of duty and gratitude counteracting… I resolved to wait on God for relief, and He was pleased to encourage my hope and trust; which made me press after further deliverance."

He sets aside time in the day for meditation and prayer and records,

> "He made me see and believe His willingness to receive into favour a poor returning prodigal, and sweetly allured and constrained my soul to stoop to Jesus' government and righteousness, to desire earnestly that my will might be entirely, eternally lost and resolved up into His holy and perfect will."

This understanding of his own sin and the relief of the Gospel marks his life, even at 23.

ii. His Ministry

Calder was ordained to the Christian ministry in 1740 in Ardersier, a small fishing village east of Inverness. He then moved to Croy in 1750. The record of his 10 years in Ardersier and the first 12 years in Croy are limited. But in 1762 he recorded memorandums for the benefit of his family.

Reading Calder's entries, you learn of his practice of visiting the sick, catechizing in the home, and his diligence in family worship. We also learn his heart for the Gospel. On one occasion his diary notes his dismay after witnessing an ordination sermon, saying "Nothing, alas! alas! of precious Christ and His glorious gospel in the ordination sermon."

But I wish to glean from his prayer life. Calder was acutely aware of his need to minister the Word of God with the attendance of the Holy Spirit's power. And he knew this came by prayer.

> Dec 4, 1762 — "Close at study all day. Some materials prepared; but oh! I fear that they are ununctioned—too much of my wretched unhallowed self in them, and too little of Christ and the Spirit. Lord, supply my deficiency according to the riches of Thy glorious grace."

> Dec 18 — "Studied all day; too little in prayer. Lord! pity, forgive, and cure my atheism and indevotion. Lord, make tomorrow a memorable day."

His writings also reflect something of what he expected of himself. Every burden—both internal and external—became a call to prayer:

> Mar 30, 1763 — "This day I have *many calls* to retire, fast, pray, and humble myself deeply before the Lord for my numberless sins of omission and commission of old and late—the situation of my parish, family, and several of my dear friends, calls for it. Lord!"

> April 15, 1763 — "This day I have *many loud calls* to be returned from the world, and devote as much of it as I possibly can to fasting, humiliation, and prayer, and that because of my little progress, or rather my lamentable deficiency in sanctification, spirituality, heavenly-mindedness, and want of preparation for death, judgment, and eternity… I have been miserably inconstant, unstable as water, variable as the wind, prone to backslide, unfaithful to my vows, unsteady in my resolutions, unthankful for signal mercies, though unworthy of the least. Oh! what a monster of ingratitude am I! Oh! what a whorish, roving, faithless, atheistical heart have I! for these let my heart bleed; for these let mine eyes mourn today."

At 9 p.m. that evening, he recorded the Lord's goodness to him as he waited in prayer.

In the following weeks and months, Calder assigns various days for humiliation and prayer. And God rewards his diligence. He recorded, "Blessed be the Lord, there is greater flocking to Christ this year than there has been for some years past."

The next year, the pattern of setting aside a day or a part of a day for prayer continues. Though he has to endure the grief of the passing of his only daughter, on the last day of 1764, he wrote:

> "This being the last day of the year, I cannot conclude these memorandums without blessing, praising, and adoring the Triune Jehovah for the miracles of His power and grace I have seen this year in the conversion of many souls; in which respect this has been the happiest year of my poor ministry."

In 1765, his workload increased, but he enjoyed more of the Lord's blessing. At the end of the year, he enters these words:

> "Blessed be His gracious name, this year has exceeded the last, happy as it was, in the number of converts... Heaven and earth praise Him for His wonderful goodness to me this year, in which I had more work than ever, and in which I was more remarkably assisted in the public than ever."

Calder's habit of prayer continued in 1766, noting on May 15, "Still I am encouraged more and more *to wait on the Lord in every emergency.*"

The mid-1760s seem to have been the highlight of his ministry, as he enjoyed a measure of local revival. However, Calder's health is failing and the greater extent of blessing fades. At the end of 1770, while he had cause to hope that his flock had been prospering in grace and advancing in holiness, he notes, "yet very few have been awakened, as far as I can judge."

The record at the end of 1771 is similar. He is critical of himself,

> "For this I have too good cause to fear that I am in a great measure to blame, as I have not been wrestling with the angel of the covenant and travailing as it were in birth, with all the ardour and agony of soul that the infinite importance of the case requires."

However, he has not given up his days of retirement. Approaching 60 years of age, we find him still retiring to meet with God. And in the final year of his life, in 1775, despite increasing weakness, God still afforded him encouragement in his ministry.

On December 11, 1775, while visiting his youngest son, Charles, James Calder took ill. He passed from the presence of his three sons into the presence of the Lord on December 24. The last words he uttered were, "He's coming, He's coming." And when one asked, "Who is coming?" he answered, "Precious Christ."

III. Some Observations

First, *his prayers were effectual for his family.* Unlike so many in the ministry, James Calder did not let the ministry hinder his duties to his family. His wife died young, leaving him with three boys and one girl, Annie, who died in 1764. Before she died, she left a clear testimony of saving grace. As for his sons, all three entered the ministry.

In a letter shortly after the death of Calder, his second son Hugh speaks of his father in a way any parent could only wish:

> "Very soon after my brother's settlement at Rosskeen, the health of the dearest, the loveliest, the most affectionate and best of parents, and best of men, began to give way… Silent is that tongue that tenderly soothed all our sorrows, and weekly counselled us in all our doubts… A more dutiful and affectionate parent never lived."

Second, *his prayers were effectual for his parish.* His diary records the burden he had for the souls God had placed under his care. One encouragement from his diary is his Sabbath evening thoughts. He often noted there were those sobbing and weeping under the influence of the preached Word.

Third, *his prayers were effectual for himself.* James Calder battled under a deep sense of his own sinfulness. Although there is not the same melancholy spirit that is notable in David Brainerd, there is a deep awareness of his own corruption. Unbelief and pride are the primary struggles. Yet, his days of retirement in prayer helped him. They not only deepened his humility, but by them he enjoyed the sweet application of the Gospel to his soul.

Every time he had reason to believe something was wrong with himself or others, he would set aside a day for prayer. In the evening after one such day he stated, "Next to the Lord's blessed days, these days of retirement and prayer, etc., have been by far the happiest of my poor life."

And that is the primary takeaway from his life.

The retirement to prayer is a *blessed retirement*. After one such day on December 18, 1766, he records,

> "Of new I set my seal to it that He is a prayer-hearing God, and that for me it is good that I draw near to God; and if any of my children after my departure shall happen to cast their eyes on these cursory memorandums, I charge them in the name of the Lord to *follow the example of their father in these sacred and blessed retirements when there is a call in Providence*—and these calls will be very frequent. I call them blessed retirements, for they have been most remarkably blessed to me for many years. On these occasions I got everything from the Lord

that my heart desired—my evidences cleared, my doubts resolved, my fears silenced, my corruptions mortified."

As we cast our eyes upon "these cursory memorandums," we also hear the charge to give ourselves to such "blessed retirements."

Experiencing challenges in your life? In your family? In your church? In your ministry? Many ills might be avoided and sweet blessings experienced if we took up this practice. May God help you embrace this lost discipline.

CHAPTER 13

How to Conduct and Contribute to a Prayer Meeting

In times of revival, prayer meetings are robust and relatively straightforward. But in tough seasons for the Church, prayer meetings prove themselves to be delicate and difficult.

So what should a church prayer meeting look like? If I had been asked that question several years ago, I would have responded with bewilderment. Not that there is only one way to do a prayer meeting, but I would have assumed it was straightforward. Experience, however, has taught me that is not the case.

When I speak of a prayer meeting, I am not referring to everyone putting their requests on a list, and the pastor prays through the list.

A prayer meeting is a gathering of saints in which the opportunity is given for any saint to pray audibly, one after another. The total time set aside is usually predetermined, although there is a place for open-ended prayer meetings that finish only when the one leading the prayer meeting believes it is time to conclude.

Not all prayer meetings are alike in their structure and purpose. But if it can be established that the Great Commission is the primary task of the Church—and I believe it can—then our prayer meetings need to reflect this task.

Before His ascension, the Lord Jesus gave His followers a mandate to make disciples in every nation. The entire world was ignorant of the Gospel, and eleven men are told to reach the world. The impossibility of the task could have been crushing.

Nevertheless, they were not dismayed. Having been commanded to do something impossible, they knew their greatest need was power. Power is precisely what Jesus promised as He ascended. "Ye shall receive power…" And that is what the apostles received after waiting for it in prayer (Acts 2:4; 4:31).

But most church prayer meetings are nothing like this, even in churches led by men that understand the need for the Holy Spirit's power.

So, how do we, with the Lord's help, make the most of the corporate seasons of prayer?

1. Conducting Prayer Meetings

First, *there is a need for education* (Ps. 44:1; Ps. 78:1–6).

In most prayer meetings, the only education experienced (aside from any preaching that occurs) comes as prayer requests, in which we learn the details of various needs. I recommend that you fight the temptation to share prayer requests. If there is something pressing and relevant to everyone in the meeting, the pastor will often know about it and can choose whether to share it. Teach God's people that if there is a burden on their heart, then mention it in prayer. Everyone will be informed and will pray with them, with the additional benefit that it will give more time for prayer itself.

Rather than a list of prayer requests, the best education we can receive often comes from recounting history. It is a powerful thing to come before God with a deep understanding of church history, and a knowledge of the mighty acts of God in the past.

For that reason, it is appropriate for those that oversee prayer meetings to share historical accounts of revival. Prayers are often tied to what we believe God can do. Thus, congregations need their vision broadened and deepened. For example, they need to know that there is such an experience as genuine revival—personal and corporate revival, as well as national revival. If they do not know, they will never ask for it.

This approach has precedent in history, such as the Cambuslang revival in 1742, and the Dundee revival in 1839. In both cases, the ministers (William M'Culloch and Robert Murray M'Cheyne, respectively) read historical accounts of God's blessing to their people in the months and years leading up to the revivals.

Second, *there is a need for application*. Not all church prayer meetings will have preaching, but if the setting allows for it, preach the Word.

However, do not turn the meeting into a Bible study. It is a prayer meeting, so the objective is to facilitate prayer. The sermon should not be similar to a Lord's Day exposition. The goal is different. Thus, the sermon is best when tailored so as to lead people to pray for power to fulfill the Great Commission. Leave other subjects alone if you wish to have a good prayer meeting.

I received this advice from Alan Cairns many years ago—a man that had a huge influence upon my life and ministry. Aside from being an excellent theologian, Cairns was gifted at leading prayer meetings. He would often speak extemporaneously and moved the congregation into a frame of mind prepared for prayer. In a lengthy discussion about various subjects just before my ordination, Cairns urged me to not turn the prayer meeting into a Bible study. He was of the opinion that Bible studies killed prayer meetings and distracted from the primary objective of intercessory prayer for lost souls, and the fulfilling of the Great Commission. I believe he was correct, and have sought to follow his counsel.

Third, *there is a need for specification*. Try to maintain a clear focus in every prayer meeting. If you are there to fast and pray for the nation, then leave other matters for another time. Consider Acts 12:5, "Peter therefore was kept in prison: but prayer was made without ceasing of the church unto God for him." The focus of the Church was to pray for Peter and nothing else mattered. It is your responsibility, as the leader, to set the direction of the prayer meeting by your preaching and preliminary comments. Take your duty seriously. Good leadership can make all the difference in a prayer meeting. In addition, teach and model what follows under the next heading.

II. Participating in Prayer Meetings

It was Charles Spurgeon who said, "We shall never see much change for the better in our churches in general till the prayer meeting occupies a higher place in the esteem of Christians."[53]

But not only do we need to esteem the prayer meeting, we need to protect it. Prayer is difficult because it is spiritual. In addition, Satan works against prayer meetings and is the master of distraction (Acts 16:16–18).

So, if you are a participant in a prayer meeting, what are some things to keep in mind?

First, *your prayers should be scriptural.* There is no greater motivator to prayer than the Word of God. As individuals, we should come to the place of prayer with scriptural arguments. We can bring no stronger plea than, "Lord, thou hast said…" This is what the psalmist does in Psalm 119:49, "Remember the word unto thy servant, upon which thou hast caused me to hope."

Years ago, I used to pray with an older gentleman. I still remember the first time I heard him pray. I was sitting in our church's 8 a.m. Lord's Day prayer meeting. By the time this man finished his prayer, I felt like I was sitting in heaven with the Lord.

And that experience with this man was not a freak event. What was the secret? Obviously, his own walk with God was foundational. But I realized the thing that set his prayers apart from almost everyone else was his use of Scripture. Whatever he had been reading and meditating upon would frame the direction of his prayer. Passages —sometimes obscure to many believers—would be intertwined into his petitions before God.

You may not get to the place this man did, but the principle is the same. When others hear the Scriptures rehearsed before God, the Holy Spirit rallies everyone around God's Word. Quoting Scripture increases faith and strengthens expectation. So learn to pray God's Word.

Second, *your prayers should be eternal*. A fast way to kill the vision of a local church is to focus most of the prayers on temporal matters. Do not misunderstand me, there is a place for praying for physical needs, financial needs, difficult circumstances, etc. However, we cannot afford to lose sight of the pressing need for the conversion of souls, the edification of saints, the raising up of laborers for the kingdom, the revival of the Church, etc.

Our prayer meetings need to have a heavy focus on matters of eternal significance.

The denomination in which I minister commenced in 1951, and has a deep history when it comes to the practice of corporate prayer. However, even with a rich heritage and the influence of former generations, it is a battle to maintain a focus on the eternal. In a sermon preached after his retirement, I heard one of our denomination's most esteemed ministers, Alan Cairns, say,

"There is a deadness in our prayer meetings. It used to be that there was a pleading with God in prayer, a passionate pleading with God. A holding up of the promises of God. Where the prayer meeting wasn't all taken up with health and wealth. Now I believe in praying for the sick. I believe in being compassionate to the needy. But men and women, there is a greater burden. Our land is going to hell, our nation is under judgment, our churches are facing the greatest challenge they have ever faced since the days of the reformation and we are at our weakest point. We need to get through to God. There has to be a pleading. A yearning. A burning out in prayer. The burden that Knox had when he looked at Scotland and he cried, 'God, give me Scotland, or I die!'"

I have been in many prayer meetings where God has come down, but they are too infrequent. Much of our praying lacks a deep spiritual burden, as seen in the above prayer of John Knox.

If we believe that men and women without Christ will suffer forever in the fires of God's hell, we would not need to be told of the priority to pray for them. While we assent to the Bible's doctrine of eternal punishment, in practice we often deny it. God help us!

Third, *your prayers should be personal*. There is a two-fold reason that your corporate praying should have a personal element to it. One is to help with brevity, and the other is to fuel intensity.

Unless you are engaged in an extended season of prayer with a handful of people, your audible prayers in a prayer meeting are best when you are brief. Seven people can take up almost 50 minutes by praying for 7 minutes each—which is not a long time. We need to exercise brevity so more people can participate.

If you want to pray for everyone you know in need, and for every matter you know needs prayer, God bless you. But I recommend that you do it at home. To quote Charles Spurgeon, "It is dreadful to hear a brother or sister pray us into a good frame of mind and heart, and then, by their long prayer, pray us out of it again."[54]

For this reason, before you open your mouth, prioritize your burdens. Take only one or two to mention audibly in prayer. Some of the best prayer meetings I have ever experienced were marked by the fact that nearly everyone prayed, and they focused on one or two matters each.

In addition, if you keep your prayers relating to matters you are personally concerned about, you will pray with more intensity. Everyone can tell the difference between prayers you *want* to pray and prayers you *need* to pray. Again, Spurgeon said, "Oh! brothers and sisters, one warm, hearty prayer is worth twenty of those packed in ice. I fear that much of our prayer is lost because we don't sufficiently throw our hearts into it."[55]

More could be said, but the main takeaway is that we can stifle prayer meetings by not understanding what we are attempting to do. By good leadership and participation, prayer meetings can become a place for some of the most memorable occasions in your local church.

If your church does not have a prayer meeting, I urge you to reconsider. Do not stop because only 5% of your membership attends. That is an enlightening statistic, because it helps you understand the spiritual temperature of your people. Red-hot Christians do not miss prayer meetings. Period. Thus, without the prayer meeting, you might be deluded regarding the health of your congregation. When only 5% turn up, press on and pray for the revival your church evidently needs.

Conclusion

I end as I began. Sometimes in life you need to start over. Not that we need to be saved all over again. But what is true of the Church in this life, is true of the Christian—we cannot die, but our spiritual life can and does decay.

I see two errors almost everywhere I look. On the one hand, there is despair for the state of the Church. And on the other, there is a delusional contentment.

It is impossible to ignore the spiritual exertion that preceded revivals in the past. Can such resolute Christians be found in the Church today? Every revival emerges when a handful of believers get extraordinarily earnest. They want nothing but God. Such Christians become convinced, "thy lovingkindness is better than life" (Ps. 63:3).

For Christ's honor, these Christians believe that the world needs the Church to offer more prayer, exhibit more holiness, and engage with greater earnestness in the Great Commission. Since revival results in a dramatic advance in all these areas, they give themselves to pray for it.

These earnest Christians will pray for an hour every day with only one thing on their hearts—revival. They will meet with other believers an evening each week and pray together for one thing—revival.

When after a year of persevering in this course and revival has not come, these Christians double down. They pray two hours a day for revival and meet several evenings each week to plead before God. "They go from strength to strength, every one of them in Zion appeareth before God" (Ps. 84:7).

The publishing of this volume will be worth every effort if something on the pages ignites just one heart in such a way that leads to revival.

Perhaps that person is you? Here is what I encourage you to do:

1. Set aside one segment of your day to pray for revival (keeping in mind that any secret sin will make prayer a vain exercise). Do not worry about the time you spend in prayer at this stage. Just set aside a meeting with God for this one issue, whether it be 5 minutes or 2 hours.

2. Attend prayer meetings at your local church. In addition, find at least one like-minded believer and meet with them—at minimum—once every two weeks to pray. Endeavor to encourage each other to keep praying for revival.

3. Do not fall into the trap of believing you need more people to join you to make your time in prayer worthwhile. Be slow to introduce others unless you are convinced they understand your burden for revival.

4. Read historical accounts of revival to keep the fire burning and strengthen your desire and sense of expectation.

5. Finally, enjoy every season of prayer. If at any point seeking God feels like bondage, step back, rest, and reevaluate your motive. This should not be a drudgery. God is joy Himself. Communion with Him should not be a miserable experience, unless He is putting His finger on our sin. But even that uncomfortable encounter is followed by the consolation of forgiveness. In short, when fellowship with God is enjoyed, time in His presence is worth it whether or not you see revival.

Whatever you do with your life, do not die having never prayed in earnest for a *breath from heaven*.

Endnotes

1. Edwards, Jonathan. The Works of Jonathan Edwards, vol. 2. (Edinburgh: Banner of Truth, 1976), 265.
2. The Revival of Religion. (Edinburgh: Banner of Truth, 1984), 11.
3. Campbell, Duncan. The Price and Power of Revival. (1956).
4. Pierson, Arthur. The Missionary Review of the World, vol. 23. (New York: Funk & Wagnalls, 1910), 14.
5. Paisley, Ian. The Fifty Nine Revival. (Belfast: Valiant Press, 1969), 156–162.
6. Spurgeon, Charles. Lectures to My Students. (Peabody: Hendrickson, 2016), 50.
7. Bounds, Edward McKendree. EM Bounds, The Classic Collection on Prayer. (Orlando: Bridge-Logos, 2001), 50.
8. Edwards, Jonathan. The Works of Jonathan Edwards, vol. 1. (Edinburgh: Banner of Truth, 1976), 189.
9. Tozer, Aiden. The Pursuit of God. (Taylors: SermonAudio.com, 2017), 39.
10. Tozer. The Pursuit of God, 38.
11. Sedgwick, Obadiah. The Anatomy of Secret Sins. (Morgan: Soli Deo Gloria, 1995), 18.
12. Winslow, Octavius. Personal Declension and Revival of Religion in the Soul. (Edinburgh: Banner of Truth, 2021), 2.
13. Taylor, Howard. Hudson Taylor's Spiritual Secret. (Chicago: Moody, 2009), 246–247.
14. Winslow. Personal Declension, 1.
15. Church News: Free Church. (Stornoway Gazette, December 9, 1949).
16. Bonar, Andrew. Memoirs of McCheyne. (Chicago: Moody, 1948), xxi.
17. Lloyd-Jones, Martyn. The Modern Philistine. Accessed October 13, 2022. https://www.mljtrust.org/sermons-online/genesis-26-17-18/
18. Gill, John. An Exposition of the Old Testament, vol. 5, The Baptist Commentary Series (London: Mathews and Leigh, 1810), 345.
19. Dallimore, Arnold. George Whitefield, vol. 1. (Edinburgh: Banner of Truth, 2019), 19–25.
20. Swinnock, George. The Works of George Swinnock, vol. 1. (Edinburgh: Banner of Truth, 1992), 118.
21. Bonar. Memoirs of McCheyne, 437–438.
22. Bonar. Memoirs of McCheyne, 439.
23. The Biblical Repertory and Princeton Review, vol. 7. (Philadelphia: James A. Peabody, 1835), 216.
24. Olford, Stephen. Heart-Cry for Revival, rev. ed. (Memphis: EMI Books, 1987), 86-95.
25. Winslow. Personal Declension, 182.
26. Lloyd-Jones, Martyn. Revival. (Wheaton: Crossway, 2004), 225.
27. Murray, Iain. 2006. What Can We Learn From John Knox? Accessed October 13, 2022. https://banneroftruth.org/us/resources/articles/2006/what-can-we-learn-from-john-knox/

28	Carré, Ernest G. Praying Hyde: Apostle of Prayer. (Alachua: Bridge-Logos, 2009), 75.
29	Carré. Praying Hyde, 76.
30	Carré. Praying Hyde, 12.
31	Bunyan, John. The Pilgrim's Progress. (Fearn: Christian Focus, 2016), 80.
32	Carré. Praying Hyde, 12.
33	Gillies, John. Accounts of Revival. (Edinburgh: Banner of Truth, 1981), 198–199.
34	Wikipedia. 2005. Christianity in Korea. Last modified August 23, 2022. Accessed October 13, 2022. https://en.wikipedia.org/wiki/Christianity_in_Korea
35	Answers In Genesis. 2020. Explosive Church Growth in Iran. Accessed October 13, 2022. https://answersingenesis.org/christianity/explosive-church-growth-in-iran-reports-say/
36	Edwards. The Works of Jonathan Edwards, vol. 1, 391.
37	Macnicol, D.C. Master Robert Bruce. (Edinburgh: Banner of Truth, 2019), 188.
38	Lennie, Tom. Land of Many Revivals. (Fearn: Christian Focus, 2015), 54.
39	Moody-Stuart, Kenneth. Brownlow North: The Story of His Life and Work. (London: Hodder and Stoughton, 1879), 106.
40	Edwards. The Works of Jonathan Edwards, vol. 1, 347.
41	Huxley, Aldous. Letters of Aldous Huxley, ed. Grover Smith. (New York and Evanston: Harper & Row, 1969), 604-605.
42	Edwards. The Works of Jonathan Edwards, vol. 1, 348.
43	Prime, Samuel. The Power of Prayer. (Edinburgh: Banner of Truth, 2009), 170.
44	Matthew Henry. Matthew Henry's Commentary on the Whole Bible: Complete and Unabridged in One Volume (Peabody: Hendrickson, 1994), 959.
45	Edwards, The Works of Jonathan Edwards, vol. 2, 316–317.
46	Edwards, The Works of Jonathan Edwards, vol. 2, 323–325.
47	Whitefield, George. The Works of the Reverend George Whitefield, vol. 1. Letter CLX.
48	Knox, John. The History of the Reformation of Religion in Scotland (Glasgow: Blackie & Son, 1336), 485.
49	Fleming, Robert. The Fulfilling of Scripture, vol. 1. (Glasgow: Young, 1801), 384–385.
50	Spurgeon, Charles. The Dawn of Revival Speedily Answered, Metropolitan Tabernacle Pulpit, vol. 13.
51	Murray, Iain. Evangelicalism Divided (Edinburgh: Banner Of Truth, 2012), 316.
52	Diary of James Calder (Banner of Truth Magazine, Issue 130, July–August, 1974). All remarks on James Calder's life are taken from this source.
53	Spurgeon, Charles. 5 Kinds of Revival the Church Needs Today. Accessed October 13, 2022. https://www.monergism.com/5-kinds-revival-church-needs-today
54	Spurgeon, Charles. Prayer Meetings. Accessed October 13, 2022. https://ccel.org/ccel/spurgeon/sermons60/sermons60.xxxv.html
55	Spurgeon. Prayer Meetings. Accessed October 13, 2022. https://ccel.org/ccel/spurgeon/sermons60/sermons60.xxxv.html